'A great guide to the wonde[
ties of being a Christian grar
and, above all, both helpful

Revd Canon J.John, evange

'Grandparents are among the most significant spiritual influences in children's and teenagers' lives. Becky Sedgwick's brilliant book not only brings encouragement to grandparents, but solid equipping. This book is hopeful, realistic and deeply relevant to every grandparent, whether their grandchildren are babies, or adults with babies of their own. Best spiritual grandparenting book I have ever read!'

Rachel Turner, founder of Parenting for Faith

'*Grandparenting for Faith* is a liberating, convicting and exciting work. It will empower grandparents in all types of family settings and dynamics to be part of their grandchildren's lives and share their faith without damaging relationships with their adult children. Read and share this book, and learn how easy it is to answer God's call to grandparent for faith.'

Martha Flavell, children and family lead at Bible Society

'*Grandparenting for Faith* is packed full of practical ideas, and it breaks things down in a clear way that will leave grandparents encouraged by what they are already doing, equipped to be more intentional, and inspired that what they are doing will make a difference in the lives of their grandchildren.'

Olly Goldenberg, founder of Children Can

'In these times of significant pressures among families, limited family time, low confidence among grandparents, confusion about roles within families and limited availability of support for families, this book is a very welcome tool. Beautifully written and very easy to read, it conveys a great awareness of the challenges of real life, while also prompting and encouraging grandparents to think beyond what they currently do and consider how they could develop their spiritual support of their grandchildren. I love this book. It is so much needed and I highly recommend it to all Christian grandparents who want to see their faith passed on to their children and grandchildren.'

Sarah Holmes, researcher and lecturer, Liverpool Hope University

Grandparenting for Faith

Sharing God with the
children you love the most

Becky Sedgwick

BRF
Ministries

 **Ministries**

15 The Chambers, Vineyard
Abingdon OX14 3FE
brf.org.uk

Bible Reading Fellowship (BRF) is a charity (233280)
and company limited by guarantee (301324),
registered in England and Wales

ISBN 978 1 80039 204 5
First published 2024
10 9 8 7 6 5 4 3 2 1 0
All rights reserved

Text by Becky Sedgwick 2024
This edition © Bible Reading Fellowship 2024
Cover image © caanebez/stock.adobe.com

The author asserts the moral right to be identified as the author of this work

Acknowledgements

Unless otherwise stated, scripture quotations are taken from The Holy Bible, New
International Version (Anglicised edition) copyright © 1979, 1984, 2011 by Biblica. Used by
permission of Hodder & Stoughton Publishers, a Hachette UK company. All rights reserved.
'NIV' is a registered trademark of Biblica. UK trademark number 1448790.

Scripture quotations marked CEV are taken from the Contemporary English Version. New
Testament © American Bible Society 1991, 1992, 1995. Old Testament © American Bible
Society 1995. Anglicisations © British & Foreign Bible Society 1996. Used by permission.

Scripture quotations marked CEB are copyright © 2011 by Common English Bible.

Scripture quotations marked GNT are taken from the Good News Bible published by The Bible
Societies/HarperCollins Publishers Ltd, UK © American Bible Society 1966, 1971, 1976, 1992,
used with permission.

Every effort has been made to trace and contact copyright owners for material used in
this resource. We apologise for any inadvertent omissions or errors, and would ask those
concerned to contact us so that full acknowledgement can be made in the future.

A catalogue record for this book is available from the British Library

Printed and bound by CPI Group (UK) Ltd, Croydon CR0 4YY

This book is dedicated to the memory of my mother, Joan Sedgwick, who loved being a grandparent and who would have loved to have seen this book.

Contents

II
THE GRANDPARENTS' TOOLKIT

III
HELPING GRANDCHILDREN CONNECT
AND CHEERING THEM ON

Painting poppies

One day I was watching a video of an artist creating a water-colour picture. This one taught you how to create a painting of a field of poppies. I watched, fascinated, as the artist dropped odd splatters of colours and dots here and there on the blurry canvas. Gradually, as different splashes were added and gaps filled in, all those individual spots and dots emerged into a coherent picture. What began as a seemingly random collection of marks on the canvas started to join up and reveal a beautiful and striking painting of poppies.

Discipleship is like that. Think about how Jesus taught his twelve disciples. There were no systematic Bible classes, memory verses or sermon series. It started with an invitation: follow me (Matthew 9:9). And then, as they did life together, odd bits of learning happened here and there. They saw how Jesus took care to spend time with his Father. They watched as he healed. They had chats about who is the greatest, and what being a disciple really meant. They ate together and tramped the length of the country. They heard Jesus teaching, and they laughed as he outwitted the Pharisees. And they saw him in the depths of despair as the cost of following God's purpose for his life became horribly and painfully clear that first Easter.[1] Gradually all those individual conversations, experiences and observations joined up into a beautiful and coherent picture of who God is and who he wants us to be, enabling the disciples to emerge as confident and committed followers of Jesus.

If you've picked up this book, chances are it's because you have a longing to disciple your grandchildren; to help them meet and know the God whom you love. But you might not feel you know how to do that. As grandparents, it's unlikely that you see your grandchildren every day, have control over their church attendance or are fully aware of what's happening in their lives. Jesus may seem to be totally present in their homes, totally absent or something in between. You may lack confidence that you can pass on faith to your grandchildren, or you might just not see them very much. You may worry about what your grandchild's parents think about your faith or whether you have even got permission to talk about it. You may feel like you aren't a good enough Christian or know enough to help your grandchildren learn about God, or you may worry that there are so many other influences shouting loudly in their lives that your little contribution won't make a difference.

Sometimes, when we long for people we love to meet and know God, we can feel stuck. Some of you might feel your grandchildren are so very far from God, living in an agnostic family, caught up with their social life or struggling to make sense of their parents' nasty separation. You might wonder how your limited time and influence can help them. However, God doesn't expect you to solve or even understand everything. He's working all the time to bring his kingdom into those situations. Your role is to check in with him and discover your next steps. You may know immediately what your next step is, or it may simply be to pray, to watch and to wait, and then, when you see your next step, to take it. So throughout this book, you'll see some prompts to help you explore with God what your next steps might be.

As you read this book, take heart! Remember the poppies. Discipling your grandchildren is simply about journeying alongside them and helping them gradually paint a picture of who God is and who he wants them to be, and encouraging them to meet and know him for themselves. Every time you share a story about who God is, or point out what God is doing, or let your grandchildren see you connecting with God yourself, you're dropping another splash of colour on to their canvas. You might not be able to paint the whole picture for them, but your splashes of colour will join splashes other people and God himself are adding.

This book takes the proven tools and skills taught in Parenting for Faith and equips you to use them as a grandparent.

The first part of the book will help you discover how you are part of God's plan for your grandchildren's discipleship, whether they are babies, children, teens or adults, and covers some important truths that grandparents need to know. The second part, the grandparent's toolkit, shares some simple ways you can help your grandchildren meet and know God – from why prayer is the bedrock of all we do, through to how to explain who God is or show how he impacts your life. We end with part three, where we explore how we can help grandchildren connect with God for themselves and think about how we can cheer them on.

You may already be helping your grandchildren to meet and know God and, if so, we are going to encourage you and give you some additional, practical ideas. If this is new to you, or even just a dream, we'll introduce you to ideas to get you started and a host of ways that might work in your family and situation. If your grandchildren are younger, we've included suggestions for using the ideas with babies and toddlers. If your grandchildren are older, or even flown the nest, this book is full of ideas for them too. This book is for you all.

Grandparents are an integral part of God's plan for children's discipleship. Whatever your circumstances, whatever your family situation, if you are grandparenting, you can grand-parent for faith.

You've got this!

Remember the poppies. One splash at a time.

I

Truths grandparents need to know

The world of grandparenting is many and varied. You may have just one tiny bundle of joy or be overrun with tots and teens. You may feel confident or be appalled at the idea of having a degree of responsibility for another generation. You may be too involved or not involved enough. You might see eye to eye with your grandchildren's parents or feel out on a limb. You might be living next door or thousands of miles away.

There are so many variables. There's no one portrait of a grandparent today.

But there are God-truths that apply to all grandparents.

1

God invented grandparents

God knows what families need. That's why he invented grandparents. Grandparents are part of God's design for families and are central to helping grandchildren of all ages meet and know God.

Grandparents bring all sorts of extras to a family. They are an essential part of the web of support that parents and children need around them in order to flourish. They also have a unique connection with their family that gives them insight; their life experiences bring wisdom; their love brings compassion and a desire to be involved. Simply because you are a grandparent, you are important and influential and one of the most important gifts a family can have.

How children – and grandchildren – meet and know God

From the moment you learn you are to be a grandparent, your world changes. The wonder of a new life, a new generation, becomes part of your life again and as you watch your grandchildren grow, you find yourself dreaming dreams for them. You want the best for them: not just health and happiness, but a deep desire that they discover good paths, grow in confidence and character, and fulfil all that promise you see in them. You simply want the best for them in every aspect of their lives.

For those of us who are Christians, the best will always include meeting and knowing the God who makes such a difference to our lives. We know that to truly flourish, grandchildren need to know that all Jesus' promises are for them – that they are loved, guided and held by God and that they can have confidence in him and find purpose in him, whatever life looks like. God offers us so much more than just knowing *about* him; he wants us to *know* him, as a friend, a father, a saviour, a comforter and so much more. When we know him, we can access all those good things he has for us. How wonderful to be able to help your grandchildren meet and know this God too.

The good news is that you don't have to be limited to dreaming that for your grandchildren; you can be a part of them finding it out for themselves. How does that happen? God's plan for children and young people's discipleship is described in Deuteronomy:

> Listen, Israel! The Lord our God is the only true God! So love the Lord your God with all your heart, soul, and strength. Memorise his laws and tell them to your children over and over again. Talk about them all the time,

whether you're at home or walking along the road or going to bed at night, or getting up in the morning. Write down copies and tie them to your wrists and foreheads to help you obey them. Write these laws on the door frames of your homes and on your town gates.
DEUTERONOMY 6:4–9 (CEV)

God's plan is that children and young people should learn about him at home because that's where ordinary life with God takes place. Children can learn about faith in Sunday school, but who is with them in the ordinary everyday bits of life – when their brother's just whacked them over the head and forgiveness is hard, or when they come home brokenhearted when their first love dumps them, or they are musing over where to go for college? It's the people God has placed around them, the people who love them and want the best for them: their parents and carers.

I wasn't aware of any overt influence… but grandma's quiet faith and her willingness to be involved in Christian things my parents were running just added to the sense that for many of the significant grown-ups in my life a relationship with God was normal, church attendance was important and prayer impacted homelife, decision-making and coping with life events.

Children can learn about God in the most ordinary parts of life. The Bible is full of times when God met people when they were going about their ordinary every day: Gideon was threshing grain when God showed up to talk to him;

Abraham was sitting outside his tent; Samuel was tucked up in bed; Manoah's wife was in the fields; Peter was dreaming in the sun; Hagar was weeping; Moses was looking after his father-in-law's sheep.[2] In the passage from Deuteronomy, God talks about bedtimes and walks and the morning rush; we could add cleaning the kitchen, a family spat, agonising over which prom dress to buy, consoling a child whose toy has broken, rushing to the supermarket to pick up tea, visiting grandad, decorating the house for Christmas, going out for the day, or any scenario you care to add. That's where children and young people can learn about God, because that's where he is.

You might be looking at that passage and thinking: 'But isn't this just for the parents? After all, they are the ones with the kids day to day?' You might think so, but God's plan is smarter than that. To discover why, we need to take a look at what society was like when God gave these instructions.

For most of human history, family groups have lived close together, intricately involved across the generations. In Moses' time, generations were in the same tent, or in clusters of tents, raising children and grandchildren side by side. When God said, 'Talk about them when you sit at home and when you walk along the road, when you lie down and when you get up' (v. 7, NIV), he wasn't just talking to the parents; he was talking to the extended family – that big group who did day-to-day life together, who would see the children in different contexts, share in the childcare, play with them, show them how to do the chores. God was speaking to everyone involved in the children's care because he knew it was both the immediate and extended family that would be able to help the children meet him and know him in the ordinary, everyday bits of life.

He was talking about families sharing faith just like they share everything else children need to know. Children learn passions, skills and values from their families every day, without any formal structures to do that. They watch and learn, discard some things and pick up others, as they are shaped into adults. Just for a moment, think back to when you were a child. What did you learn from your grandparents? Are there things that you still do today that you picked up from them? Whether or not we are aware of it, we are shaped by our families, including our grandparents.

Think about the passion some people have for trains. Where did that come from? So often, it's from a parent or grandparent, enthusiastically taking

We talk to God just as if he's another member of our family, another person in the room. Living life drip-feeding God into it, because that's what life with God is like.

their toddler to see a steam train or spending hours playing trains on the living room floor. Children of fervent football fans absorb the game; children growing up in one of those homes where hospitality is valued and practised learn to welcome and include and be hospitable themselves. Most of the education we give our children and grandchildren is like that. We don't sit them down and give them a lesson in steam-train engineering or the value of hospitality. It happens as we go through life together, sometimes deliberately drip-feeding, the rest of the time just being ourselves and doing what comes naturally.

That's exactly how God's designed faith to be shared from one generation to the next. Drip fed, absorbed and seen in our everyday, up-and-down, ordinary lives.

But what about today? Does that plan still work? After all, our society is very different.

God's plan today is the same.

His plan is still that parents, carers and their extended family and friends are the people who will share faith with children and young people and help them to meet and know God. How that happens might look different, but it's the same principle.

But many of us – parents, carers and grandparents – have lost confidence in our ability to do that. Grandparents might feel too far away or think they don't know enough about God or the Bible. Many of us have come to see the church as the expert, the place where our children and grandchildren can learn about God and be discipled. But that's not God's view. Churches are wonderful places, full of people whose jobs and

> *Being a grandparent gives you an automatic status with your grandchildren; you are 'up on a pedestal'… So as a Christian grandparent, it gives you opportunities to influence them – just because you are their grandparent.*

gifting are to explain the Bible and who God is and to answer the big questions. But they are no substitute for the learning that takes place in the family. The Covid pandemic reminded us of something we might have forgotten: the church *can't* be central to children's discipleship. Once the church's doors closed, no matter how hard they tried, pastors, children's leaders and youth workers struggled to disciple the children and young people they were used to seeing week in, week out. But their parents, carers and family and friends could, because they were still doing day-to-day life with their children.

Discipleship starts in the home, from the moment a child is born – or even before. The church has a part to play, but it's not the main part. It's not even as important a part as grandparents, because look where you fit into God's plan: it's where you always have been, right alongside the parents and carers. Yes, there are challenges of distance, time and family dynamics, but you are the people God has placed around parents and carers to support, care and nurture them and their children. Because you know your grandchildren, have wisdom and love to offer them, and are part of their ordinary, everyday lives, whatever that looks like for you, the Bible tells us that you are part of God's design for discipling your grandchildren.

But in this modern world, with all its complexities, can grandparents still play their part in sharing faith, helping their grandchildren meet and know God?

The answer is a resounding 'Yes'.

What research tells us

Grandparents seem to have a particular role to play in families. They aren't just a second pair of hands to help with
child-rearing. Their presence is a link with the past, with
family history, values and traditions to pass down to the
next generations, and crucially, grandparents have a life-
time of accumulated maturity and experience that brings
so much to share with grandchildren just starting on their
life journeys.

Research tells us that when grandchildren feel closely
connected to a grandparent, there are a host of benefits
for those grandchildren (and often for the grandparents),
including better mental health and self-esteem; improved
resilience and a better sense of self; and more pro-social
behaviour and better peer relationships.[3] Karl Pillemer,
of Cornell University, reported that 'as many as 9 out of
10 adult grandchildren feel their grandparents influenced
their values and behaviors'.[4] In short, grandparents have
enormous potential to influence their grandchildren – for
the better. Simply by existing and being known, who you
are and what you do influences your grandchildren.

But is this still the case when it comes to influencing grandchildren spiritually?

The Bible seems to suggest so. Lois, the grandmother of
Timothy, is specifically commended by Paul as a grandma
of faith. Isaac lived with his parents and his grandfather
Abraham as a child and young teen. Jacob blessed his

grandsons, Manasseh and Ephraim, sharing with them who God was and had been for him. Naomi 'cared for' her grandson Obed, who in turn became the grandfather of King David.[5] Job 12:12 reminds us that 'wisdom is found among the aged', and Psalm 92 asserts that even in old age we can still 'bear fruit' (v. 14).

Again, modern research backs this up. Vern Bengtson, in *Families and Faith*, laid out the findings of his longitudinal research on how faith is transmitted in families. Beginning in 1970, the researchers followed more than 350 families (involving more than 3,500 individuals) for the next 35 years to find out how faith is, or is not, passed down from one generation to the next. As part of this, they noted 'the unexpected importance of grandparents': regardless of the parents' faith, grandparents can be highly significant in the development of faith in their grandchildren. They may be reinforcing the parents' influence or helping faith skip a generation when the parents don't have faith themselves.[6]

In 2016, Youth For Christ commissioned a survey of 1,001 young people, asking them questions about their culture and experiences. What it revealed about young people and faith was fascinating. When asked 'What or who influences you about faith/religion?', 73% said it was their family. Nothing else came close: teachers and friends ranked

My nan was the only Christian in my family, and now I'm a Christian I understand her influence through her actions. But at the time I didn't get it! I wonder if she prayed for me; I think she did.

both at 36%, and TV and the media 23%. Families – including grandparents – are hugely influential in the development of young people's faith. Research by others agrees. Grandparents do have influence on their grandchildren's faith – even when the parents do not have or encourage faith in those same grandchildren.[7]

Moreover, it appears that the spiritual influence of grandparents runs much deeper and lasts much longer than we might think. Susan Longhurst set out to investigate why adults converted to Catholicism and discovered that for many who had not found faith as children or young people, childhood memories of their grandparents' faith were powerful and had the ability to awaken and inspire a new faith journey many years later.[8]

As part of the research for this book, we surveyed over 300 grandchildren of Christian grandparents to see if we could discover why and how Christian grandparents had impacted their faith, and we saw the same truths in their comments:

> I can now see that my late nan supported other people and was supported by them, in her church, and it gave her purpose and connection. As I return to Christianity my nan is an example I follow.

> I saw strength, peace and contentment in the way my surrogate grandmother conducted her life. She loved her God and my mother and I knew it.

As an adult (my grandpa passed away when I was 19), I now think about how he modelled a serving heart which has massively influenced how I get involved in church and community.

I saw the way my grandmother's behaviour and approach to life was in accordance with the faith she professed. I wanted to be like that.

I saw the strength and comfort faith brought my grand-parents, which encouraged me to explore my own faith as an adult.

So that's truth number one. Grandparents are spiritually influential in the lives of their grandchildren and have huge potential to be part of their grandchildren's faith journeys. Simply because you are a grandparent, God has positioned you so you can help your grandchildren meet and know God.

2

Connection is key

In 2009 the University of Oxford produced a fascinating piece of research for the charity Grandparents Plus. Surveying 1,566 teenagers about their experiences of being grandchildren, researchers found that the majority of the teens seemed to long for a deeper and more complex relationship with their grandparents than we might assume. They wanted to share special times, like holidays and outings, with their grandparents and to have quality time alone with them. They also wanted regular contact with their grandparents, including via phone calls, emails and letters – and, 15 years later, we would add text messaging and video calls. They wanted their grandparents to be involved in their lives, being able to build trust and be vulnerable, as well as sharing interests and hearing grandparents' stories.[9]

Grandchildren and grandparents just seem to be set up to connect well: there's an expectation of love and interest from children, which means that even if they regard every other

> *I loved getting big hugs from my overjoyed-to-see-me Grandpa. It still makes me think of God to remember those hugs.*

grey-haired person on the planet as irrelevant, they do crave connection with their grandparents. Grandparents, when talking about their grandchildren, will often talk about how overwhelming their love is for them; how special they are and how they love them unconditionally.[10] Everyone needs those people who just love you, accept you and are there for you; and grandparents seemed designed to fit that bill.

The importance of connection

In the previous chapter, we thought about how influential grandparents are, and we discovered that, regardless of the parents' faith, grandparents can be highly significant in the development of faith in their grandchildren. And that's wonderful news!

In our own research, it was striking how often the grand-children reported that the reason their grandparent had influenced their faith was because they had a close relation-ship. These are some of the comments we received:

I felt completely loved by Grandma, so I trusted what she told me about God and how important he was to her.

My grandfather was someone I loved and looked up to immensely. The fact that he read the Bible and took faith seriously meant that I did too.

They were always there, so stable, dependable and loving. Their door was always open, and I was always welcome.

I was very close to my grandmother, we had a strong relationship. I wanted to please her and be like her.

Because I loved them and knew they loved me. I didn't see them very much because we lived too far away but it was special to spend time together. When I became a Christian aged about eleven at a camp, my mum said I should phone Nanny straight away to tell her as it would make her so happy!

Being in a close relationship with someone who loves you enables all sorts of good things: not just the pure enjoyment of each other's company, but also the freedom to be vulnerable, the courage to trust and the willingness to learn from each other. We are ready to be influenced by people we trust and love and open to learn from their experiences and wisdom.

> *I was incredibly close to my grandmother, and sharing her faith with me was just one part of our connection.*

The closer you are to your grandchildren, the better positioned you will be to share with them all the good things you have, including meeting and knowing the God you love. Therefore, the more you can do to be connected to your grandchildren – and ensure that they feel connected to you – the better.

Building and growing connection

So if connection is key to being able to help your grand-children meet and know God, how can you build and grow your connection with your grandchildren? Feeling and being connected to grandchildren can be a lot more complex than connecting with your own children. There are the inevitable challenges of time, distance and faith. You may find that your grandchildren's conversations are peppered with ideas and words that are new to you, or that they are growing up and less keen to spend time with you. You may have adopted, fostered or step grandchildren. Your grandchildren may be neurodiverse or have particular needs. And not every family feels well-connected, and relationships can be complicated.

Whatever your situation, there are some important ideas which we are going to explore that will help you find your next step in any situation, as well as ways to build connection with your grandchildren.

Merril Silverstein and Sarah Ruiz published some research in 2006 which found there are three things that are crucial for the development of a strong connection between grand-children and their grandparents:

- the child feeling a sense of emotional closeness to their grandparent
- the child having regular contact with their grandparent
- the child viewing their grandparent as a source of social support – perceiving that their grandparent cares for them and will help them.[11]

Let's look at each of those points and think about what that might look like for you.

Emotional closeness

Being emotionally close to someone is more than an 'I love you': it's an in-my-bones knowing that I am special to you and that together, we have a unique relationship we both love and that is good for us.

If you want to build connection with your grandchildren, finding ways to let them get to know you and for you

> *All four of my grandparents modelled unconditional love and they always showed up. I have no doubt at all that I am dearly loved by them all. I believe I was able to accept God's love because I already knew what it felt like to be loved by them.*

to really get to know them will make all the difference. Of course, it's not always simple. Jenny and Geoff, grandparents we interviewed when researching this book, shared their experience of being grandparents to four adopted grandchildren. 'Trauma,' they said, 'is real and affects the children.' It may feel harder for some children to build trust and attachment. Others may struggle with controlling their emotions and present challenging behaviour. Jenny and Geoff explained how they'd had to adapt their grandparenting to the therapeutic parenting model the children's parents used, but how, over time, trust and connection with their grandchildren had grown.

Tim and Darcy Kimmel, in *Extreme Grandparenting*, describe it like this:

> If we want to be used by God to help our grandchildren develop discernment and make right choices, we need to be willing to both welcome them into our world and hang out in theirs.[12]

'Hanging out' in your grandchildren's worlds goes beyond just knowing where they go to school or coming along to watch their football match – but happily it doesn't require you to recreate your youth or join TikTok! It's about being curious: 'Show me how to play that new game you've been raving about'; 'Tell me about your new friends at school.' It's opening conversations and finding out what makes them tick. Some grandparents we talked to said they tried to have time with each grandchild individually so they could get to know them well. And in turn, grandchildren will love being welcomed into your world. One grandparent talked about sending short videos to their grandchildren during Covid which shared their ordinary days at home and out and about. Some grandparents are able to have their grandchildren stay over or take them away. Others love sharing family history, or delight in shared interests or teaching new skills. The more you get to know each other, the closer you will become.

Another important factor in emotional closeness is the feeling that the relationship is mutually beneficial. You probably tell them 'I love you', but even with very young children, you can go one step further to help them understand that your relationship is two-way. Saying, 'When you hug me, I feel so happy,' communicates even to a toddler that they bless your life just by their presence. Your slightly older grandchild will love to see that their jokes make you laugh or that the video they just sent you absolutely made your day and you can't wait for the next one. When you message your teen granddaughter to ask for her help with your latest technological dilemma, she's going to know that you value her. Finding ways to help your grandchildren know what a difference they make to your life will build this bond of mutual closeness.

Sometimes, you might find it easier to connect with some grandchildren more than others. Maybe one has a similar personality or interests to you while their sister is a bit prickly; maybe you see one set every week while the others live hundreds

> *Make an effort – put yourself out. Foster their friendships. Be different to their mum and dad. There will be opportunities for you to be a different voice than their parents', conversations they will have with you they won't have with them.*

of miles away. If that's the case, decide to proactively build connection with those other grandchildren. If you can't see an obvious way to do that, your best course of action might be to ask God for a next step. Then wait, listen and when you sense his answer, step out in faith.

Next steps: Reflect on your relationship with your grandparents. Did you feel emotionally close to them? Why, or why not? Now think about each of your grandchildren. Do you think they feel emotionally close to you? Do you feel closer to some grandchildren than others? Talk to God about how you can continue to build those bonds.

Regular contact

The second factor Silverstein and Ruiz identified as crucial for the development of a strong connection between grandparent and grandchild is regular contact.

I was chatting to some friends about this whole grandparenting for faith business, when Mike's comment floored me. 'My mum is 87,' he said, 'and she's taught herself to use WhatsApp so she can message each of the grandchildren regularly.' It wasn't so much the fact that an 87-year-old had taught herself to use WhatsApp that hit my brain: it was the image of this elderly lady, intentionally mastering technology to stay in contact with her adult grandchildren. I could instantly see the power of that, Nanna popping up on your phone just to say hello.

There are lots of ways to be regularly in contact with your grandchildren. Perhaps you already pick them up from school once a week or provide holiday childcare. You may be in the habit of a weekly call with the family, or always pop a birthday card in the post. But how can you maximise the power of being regularly in contact?

1 **Be proactive.** Don't wait for your grandchildren to be in touch first: there's great power in knowing someone cares enough about you to make the effort to be in

touch. Sometimes connect with them out of the blue: an unexpected message, invite for a drink or quick call convey the important message: I love you and I'm thinking of you. When you know a grandchild has a special day – maybe a milestone or an important appointment – let them know you've remembered and are praying for them.

2 **Be creative**. Use different ways to be in touch. Popping a card or a tiny gift in the postbox is quick and easy, but it is a source of great delight for a grandchild who rarely gets anything through the post. Technology has made contact simple; you can ping off a quick email or message. You might share a post from Facebook with a grandchild, or film a short video for them of where you've been on your holiday today. Be in touch to offer a listening ear if you know they might need that, or just to say, 'I wanted to hear your voice.'

3 **Be individual**. If you have more than one grandchild, from time to time, be in touch with each one separately. Adapt how you do that according to their age and preferences: you might find it helpful to think about what sort of things they love doing and their personalities as you plan.

The power of regular contact is in the message it conveys: you are valuable to me, and I love you. When grandchildren hear that message, it changes things.

Next steps: Think about how you are in contact with your grandchildren. Who initiates the contact? Do you contact them as part of the family or as individuals? Are there any ideas here that you might want to try?

Viewing you as a source of social support

The third element Silverstein and Ruiz found to be important for strong connection was the idea that the grandchildren knew that their grandparents didn't just love them but were available for them when they needed them.

Being a grandparent doesn't mean that you'll always love everything about your grandchildren or look forward to the exhaustion of a day's childcare. But it's so important that you let them know that, regardless of their choices or attitudes or appearance, they are welcome and loved. Because then, when they need you, they will know they can depend on you. Being a source of social support is more than just being available, or just caring. It's about the grandchild perceiving that if they need help they can turn to you, whether that's for a shoulder to cry on, a safe place or practical help or guidance, and that they will be safe and welcomed.

> *As I approached marriage, my parents were against my choice because my husband is of a different race… One Sunday, overwhelmed with the decision I was making, I went to the altar to pray. Before I knew it my grandmother was by my side. I shared my heart with her and we prayed together. My grandparents, though concerned, never rejected me or my husband and he became very close to them.*

One grandma talked about how when her three-year-old grandson fell in the park, she instinctively held him close until he stopped crying: 'I just want him to know that I will always be there for him.' As grandchildren grow older, how you communicate that will change, but let them know by your words and your deeds that you will always make time to listen and help and be there for them.

This sense of social support isn't dependent on your being wholly available to them at the drop of a hat, or physically able to help them move house, or full of incredible wisdom that will help them know what to do in all situations. It's about being there. Being willing to stop, listen and sit with them in whatever situation they find themselves. Because that is one of the most valuable things in the world.

Next steps: Do you think your grandchildren know that you always want to be there for them? How can you show them that?

3

No one said it would be easy

The third truth that grandparents need to know is that no one said it would be easy.

When we interviewed grandparents as part of the research for this book, one of the things we didn't expect was how quickly most of the interviewees told us that being a grandparent wasn't straightforward. What they explained was this: parenting is hard enough, but grandparenting is a whole different ball game. Family dynamics can be tricky: people fall ill; tragedy strikes; there are unexpected struggles or differences of opinion; and faith itself can cause issues. Families face all sorts of ups and downs, and grandparents get to watch it all play out.

There are many times when grandparents feel powerless, or hopeless, or just confused about what to do when faced with the whirling lives of their grandchildren and children – and they may also be asking: how can I help my family meet and know the love and power of God in these circumstances?

As Christians, our first port of call is always prayer. We will explore ideas and encouragement for grandparents as they pray in chapter 4, but as you face tricky situations, remember that when we pray, we access God's shelter, strength and wisdom. He truly is 'our refuge and

Life as a Christian grand-parent can be harder, because there's this extra thread of faith you are trying to thread through different situations. But as a Christian grand-parent you get to pray and share the stuff that concerns you with God.

strength, an ever-present help in trouble'.[13] Pray that God will show you your next steps as you walk alongside them: what is the one next thing I can do to help them discover who God is? Pray for God to place Christian friends and colleagues around them who can speak into their lives. Pray for yourselves, for wisdom and hope.

In part II, we'll look at some practical tools and skills grandparents can use to help share faith with their grandchildren. But first, let's take a moment to look at some common situations you might find yourself in and share some ideas that will set you up to use those skills and tools well.

When your children don't share your faith

Imagine an heirloom quilt, lovingly stitched by great-grandma, passed down to each generation. You loved it, spread it proudly over your bed every day and enjoyed the warmth it brought. And then, when the time was right, you passed it on to your child. But you soon discover that your adult child isn't using the quilt. It's not on the bed; it's packed away in a cupboard. Maybe it's brought out when you visit, or used at special occasions like Christmas. But it's just not relevant to your modern child with their own ideas and influences.

Faith can feel like that. Many of us made sure that faith was something our children knew and experienced during their childhood. They came with us to church, read their Bibles, seemed to have some sort of faith – but as they grew older, faith got pushed to the edges of their lives and maybe seemed to disappear altogether. We tried to pass on our faith, but it got packed away in a cupboard.

Your adult child might have changed their faith or married someone of another faith. You might have come to faith later in life and weren't able to bring your children up knowing God. Some might never seem to have understood faith or have rejected it, and that can feel hard.

Mary and Paul, two of the wise grandparents we interviewed, told us this: 'Know it's not all on you. You're not responsible if children and grandchildren decide not to follow Jesus – it's their free choice.' Even so, you may be grieving or feel ashamed or like you've failed. But there's good news. It's never too late for your adult children to meet God and know the joy of having him in their lives. There is always hope, because God is a God of hope.

So what can you do practically to encourage your adult children meet and know God? Everyone's family is unique and how you share faith will depend on so many factors. But here are some ideas to help you figure out your next steps.

1 **Build your relationships with your children as well as your grandchildren and love them unreservedly.** The more connected you are, the more influence you will have and the more opportunities to share who God is.

2 **Reshape your view.** The phrase 'pass on your faith' implies that it's a done deal – you've either done it or you haven't. But that's not how faith works. As Christians, we're not passing on a set of religious activities and beliefs. We're passing on a relationship with a God who, for us, has been an amazing God. If we think less about 'passing on faith' and more about 'helping someone discover who God is', then it becomes easier to see that this is something you can do as a parent of an adult child. The ideas in part II will help you with this.

3 **Reflect on the barriers.** Sometimes people struggle to know or like God because there are barriers to them doing so. If you can identify any obvious barriers, that may give you an important next step, such as explaining something that happened in the past, or apologising, or asking questions. Examples of barriers might include:

- never really understanding who God is; he just isn't relevant to me and my life
- having big questions that haven't been adequately answered, such as 'Why does God allow suffering?' or 'How can you believe in God and science?'

- being hurt by church or seeing a disconnect between what Christians say and what they do
- feeling that they aren't good enough for God because of their lifestyle, choices or past.

4 **Don't let faith become a bone of contention.** Faith – or the lack of it – is only one part of who your children are. Don't try to enforce your beliefs on them, and even if you don't agree with all their choices or opinions, try to understand their views and be gentle if you disagree.

> *Don't put pressure on faith things. Don't say, 'When are the babies going to be baptised', even if the fact they haven't been baptised is painful for you, if you sense it might not be welcome or helpful.*

When you're not allowed to talk about faith

Grace and Harry's son-in-law laid down the law: 'I will not allow you to talk about God or church with your grandchildren.' They recoiled from the shock – not just the sadness of not being able to share God with their precious grandsons, but also the practicalities of how even to talk about their church-filled lives without transgressing this rule.

Many grandparents face situations where faith is an issue with their families and sometimes any talk of God or church will be frowned upon or met with hostility or even anger.

Alongside praying for your family, in these circumstances what can grandparents do?

1 **Respect the parents' decisions and boundaries about faith matters.** Your children are now the adults, making their own choices and parenting decisions; make it clear that you respect their right to hold their views so that you don't damage your relationship with them or erode trust.

> We are careful to respect their wishes. We asked and were allowed to give our granddaughter a Bible storybook for Christmas two years ago, but weren't allowed to give her another one.

2 **Try to understand their views.** If you can, ask about their views so you can understand what motivates them and what they fear about you sharing your faith with their children. If you can, explain gently how their decision impacts you.

3 **Make it clear that they are important to you and you love them.** Family relationships can be complicated enough without faith differences. When faith is so important to you, you could accidentally alienate children who don't share your beliefs. If everyone else is joyously celebrating Easter, how can you ensure they don't feel left out? If it's Sunday and you normally go to church, but your children are visiting, how will they feel?

4 **Ask for permission before you expose your grandchildren to anything about God or church.** Perhaps explain that the Bible's an important part of

your family's heritage and so would it be okay to give your grandchild a Bible? Or would they be happy if Darcy came to the holiday Bible club at church while she's staying with you?

5 **Remember that faith isn't only communicated or demonstrated through words.** Your grandchildren will be noticing what inspires you, what your values are, how you live – and this will have an impact. God is working behind the scenes, and one day, your grandchildren will be old enough to ask you themselves about your faith.

When contact is hard

Sue sat in her homegroup and shared yet another tale of the continual bickering between her and her daughter. 'And now she won't let Ryan come round to see me!' she said. Another nanna wept as she explained that she had no idea why, but her son refused to have any contact with her at all. How can grandparents share God when you never see your grandchildren or contact is just plain hard?

1 **Pray.** The Common English Bible translation of 1 Peter 5:7 says this: 'Throw all your anxiety onto him, because he cares about you.' In such a tough situation, throw your fears, your sorrow, your grief at God. He cares for you – and for your grandchildren. One grandma we interviewed said: 'Choose not to be a worrier for your children but a prayer warrior'. Prayer is your secret weapon.

2 **Be ready to build bridges.** Family life is complicated! As you reflect on your situation, God might poke your heart about something you may have said or done that has contributed to this disconnection. If he points anything out, do be quick to offer an apology, explain things, forgive or ask for forgiveness.

3 **Prioritise connection.** We've seen how important connection is. So do all you can to re-establish or strengthen the connection you have with your children or grandchildren. Revisit the ideas in chapter 2 and see if there is anything you might want to try. By focusing on being as connected as you can to your family, you are making so much more possible.

4 **Keep asking God for your next steps, and be prepared for these to be quite ordinary.** One distressed nanna told the story of how her young granddaughter refused to have any contact with her, and she just didn't know what to do. At a grandparenting for faith group, someone suggested just asking God for her next step. A week later, Audrey came in beaming. 'God told me to invite Sophie to come with me in the car when I was going to visit her aunty,' she said, 'and she came!' That simple step changed everything.

When your family is in pain

'Ever since they moved,' Jenny said, 'Pete and Gemma just haven't settled into church and the children miss it. They really need to find a new church family.' David's eyes brimmed with tears as he described how powerless he felt when he discovered his beloved grandson had been cutting himself.

How painful it is to watch someone you love struggle. Sadly, it seems that this is a non-negotiable part of the job description for grandparents. It can feel hard to know how to make a difference – particularly for those of us who have faith, how to help your family know the love and power of God in those circumstances.

> My grandmother lost her first baby girl at eight months old, and I lost my first baby girl at birth. The fact that I knew she was praying for me and my husband with faith gave me hope and comfort. She would often remind me that she is praying that the Lord would bless us again with a child very soon, and he did!

1 **Offer what help you can – even if you can't do much.** One of the most powerful things people need when they are in trouble is to have people alongside them who will listen and hold them. Unless it will make the situation worse, always offer to pray and keep checking in with how you can pray next.

2 **Know when to interfere and when not to.** There will be times when you long to put your two-pennyworth in. But before you do, it's worth checking your motive. Is this something that's causing you real concern – the family

is arguing frequently, or the grandchildren staying out way too late and getting into trouble – or is this just about a difference in parenting style, disliking your granddaughter's dummy, or wishing your grandkids were reading books instead of being glued to a screen. If you have genuine concerns, then try to gently and non-judgementally raise them. But if it's just a difference of opinion about how to parent, don't interfere – even if it's hard not to.

3 **Be a safe place for your grandchildren.** As mentioned in chapter 2, research into the impact of grandparents on their grandchildren repeatedly reports that when a grandchild is in crisis or their family situation is difficult, the presence of a loving grandparent can make all the difference.[14] As much as you can, be available for grandchildren who may be struggling: be proactive in getting in touch; offer what you can; listen well; don't judge; and love well. You can also be a safe place for a grandchild who might worry that their lifestyle or choices might alienate them from you. As Anita Cleverley says:

> Let's choose to be such people, unshockable and unafraid of the multifarious social and sexual land-scape we all inhabit, and that will help us, whatever our grandchildren's life choices, to offer one of the most precious gifts a grandparent can give – uncon-ditional love.[15]

When you are struggling

We all struggle from time to time. Grandparents may struggle with the normal challenges of growing older, such as health problems and increasing frailty, but there can be other challenges too. One grandma talked about how debilitating it was trying to grandparent for faith when her husband was unsupportive and uninterested in God. Another grandparent related how, after her son came round to announce they were moving from down the road to 200 miles away, she was unexpectedly and profoundly struck with grief at the loss of their beloved granddaughters. Grandparenting may feel that bit harder when you are struggling yourself.

So what might help you when this happens?

1 **Remember that God's involved in all of this.** His intention has always been that grandparents are part of his design for helping grandchildren meet and know God – and that doesn't change because your situation is less than ideal. He's with you on this journey and is working all the time to bring his kingdom into those situations.

2 **Remember that God knows what you can manage.** If you are struggling, remember that God knows that. There's a beautiful picture of God in John 21 when Peter sees the resurrected Jesus for the first time. Jesus pulls his friend aside and asks him, 'Peter, do you love me?' What our English translations don't convey here is that the word Jesus uses for love is *agape*. He is asking Peter

if he loves him with that unconditional God-love. But Peter, still full of guilt from his betrayal of Jesus, can't look him in the eye. 'Jesus,' he replies, 'you know I love you' – but Peter can only promise the ordinary love for a brother – *philo*. Jesus gently repeats the question, and again, Peter is unable to say he loves Jesus with *agape* love. But then there comes a moment which brings hope to all of us who feel inadequate or unable. Jesus asks the question again, but this time starting where Peter is: 'Peter, do you *philo* me?' God knows that sometimes we can't do it all, and that's okay.

3 **Get yourself some support.** The British are renowned for their stiff upper lip, and it can feel very hard to talk freely about your families. And it might feel extra hard to open up to Christian friends if you are painfully aware that your family might not live up to the image of the perfect Christian family. But getting some support for yourself will make all the difference. Having others around us when we need help is one of the most wonderful gifts of church – because it's so hard doing it on our own. Take inspiration from the story of Moses, Aaron and Hur in Exodus 17:

> Joshua did as Moses commanded him and went out to fight the Amalekites, while Moses, Aaron, and Hur went up to the top of the hill. As long as Moses held up his arms, the Israelites won, but when he put his arms down, the Amalekites started winning. When Moses' arms grew tired, Aaron and Hur brought a stone for him to sit on, while they stood beside him

and held up his arms, holding them steady until the sun went down. In this way Joshua totally defeated the Amalekites.

EXODUS 17:10–13 (GNT)

You may already have trusted friends who are your Aaron and Hur, but if not, ask God to show you who will hold your arms up and provide the support and encouragement you need – and then be courageous enough to ask them if they will join you for a season as you grandparent for faith in whatever situation your family is in.

God's not finished with them yet

Sometimes, in family life, it can seem so hard to see or even imagine God is at work, let alone that your grandchildren might ever get to meet and know God.

Catherine had walked away from God aged 16, convinced that being gay meant that she couldn't love or be loved by God. Her family watched over the next 30 years as she forged a successful career, married her long-term partner and settled into a busy and happy life – and grieved that she seemed so far from God. And then, seemingly within the space of a few weeks, everything changed. Catherine rang her mum. 'I'm going to church,' she said. 'I've become a Christian.' Within months, she'd been baptised and had set her eyes firmly on Jesus.

Catherine's family were astounded. But as she shared her story with them, they realised that although there had been no outward signs of it, God had been steadily working in Catherine's life for years. A desire to keep her childhood Bible. Discovering Christian radio by accident when she couldn't tune in to her normal show. Questions that she longed to know the answer to.

Be encouraged. Whatever it looks like on the outside, God's not finished with your family yet. As you pray for your grand-children and their families, keep asking God for your next step. He's on the case!

11

The grandparents' toolkit

When my daughter was young, I wanted to raise her to be a Christian, so naturally I looked for advice. A friend said that her child simply loved these Bible reading notes, so I bought a copy – but it turned out that my dyslexic daughter really wasn't very excited by them. I knew that another family at my church did family devotions at breakfast every morning, but in our crazy house that just couldn't happen. I then read a book that advised me to get up early every day and pray for my daughter; I tried it once and fell asleep.

There's no one size fits all when it comes to discipling children and young people, because every family is different and every child is different. So at Parenting for Faith, we have developed a toolkit with different skills and approaches that help parents, carers and grandparents disciple children and young people.

You are the grandparent God has given to your grandchildren. Pick up and use the tools that will work for you. Our prayer is that, as you do this, they will help you find your next step as you seek to help your grandchildren meet and know God.

4

Pray, pray, pray

A few years ago, we had a new curate, who had come to faith as an adult. His parents hadn't been Christians; they had a nodding acquaintance with the local church, but faith and God were absent from Jonny's home. But one day, he said something that I've never forgotten: 'I had a praying grandmother.' I don't know whether that grandma lived long enough to see her prayers come to fruition, but I do know that many other grandparents pray, holding out hope that God will somehow break through into their grandchildren's lives.

We spoke to lots of Christian grandparents when we were researching this book. Almost every time, when we asked them what advice they'd give to other Christian grandparents, the first thing they said was 'Pray, pray, pray.' It seems that it's the natural instinct of a grandparent to pray – and when we think about what prayer is, that shouldn't be a surprise.

As Christians we sit in a world that's not at all as God intended. We see the effect of sin; we realise that not everyone knows the God who loves them. We are angered by injustice, we grieve with the hurting and we'd love to see things change. As grandparents, you long for good things for your grandchildren. You may be looking at the path ahead of them and wonder how they are going to navigate that well. You may have grandchildren who are hurting. You may simply want to help them see and know God better and to ask for his blessing and for whatever they need.

Prayer is the gift God has given us to help us make a difference. It is powerful and can break through barriers that seem impregnable. Whatever is going on in your grandchildren's life, you can pray.

What a relief! What a wonderful thing to know that whatever is going on, however little or however much you understand, God is there in the middle of it all with you, partnering with you in this so precious job

> *Just knowing my grandma was praying for me as I grew into adulthood was powerful – every card or letter was signed 'Love and prayers, Grandma'.*

of loving your grandchildren well. To partner with someone, we need to be able to communicate with them, which is why God has given us prayer – not only as a way to ask questions and receive guidance, but as a safe place to share your hopes and dreams, to celebrate or lament or just to find a place to rest and recover. Prayer is your strongest ally as you care for your grandchildren. As one grandmother said to us: 'Nobody can stop you praying for your children and grandchildren, even if you cannot pray with them.'

A Bible picture of prayer

'Hands together, eyes closed': for those of you brought up in British schools, this probably brings back memories of daily assemblies: eyes screwed tightly together, hands pointed firmly towards the chin, and the loudly chanted 'Amen' as the headteacher drew their prayer to a close. But the Bible shows us that prayer is so much more than that.

The Bible is full of stories of people praying. Jonah, faced with his rebellion, cries out to God from the belly of the fish. Jacob wrestles with God. Jesus withdraws to a quiet place to spend time with his Father. Paul speaks of our wordless prayers and the Holy Spirit's groans as he intercedes for us. Hannah weeps; Deborah celebrates; Abraham negotiates; Gideon questions.[16] There are so many pictures of prayer, but there are four which might be especially helpful as you pray for your grandchildren.

Jairus

When Jesus had again crossed over by boat to the other side of the lake, a large crowd gathered round him while he was by the lake. Then one of the synagogue leaders, named Jairus, came, and when he saw Jesus, he fell at his feet. He pleaded earnestly with him, 'My little daughter is dying. Please come and put your hands on her so that she will be healed and live.' So Jesus went with him.
MARK 5:21–24

I imagine Jairus must have been desperate. His daughter was dying; rushing from her bedside, he came and fell at the feet of the only person he knew who could possibly do something. There will be times when your grandchildren's lives might feel so terribly hard and leave you feeling like you have no idea how to help. But God does. Just like Jairus, you get to bring your grandchildren to the feet of the living and loving God, not knowing what he'll do, but confident that he cares and will take notice of you.

Ezekiel

> 'I looked for someone among them who would build up the wall and stand before me in the gap on behalf of the land.'
> EZEKIEL 22:30

In this passage, Ezekiel is talking about the wall that would have surrounded an ancient city, offering protection from the enemies who might be circling about. A breach in the wall, a gap, would make the city and its inhabitants vulnerable to attack; what it needed was someone to stand in the gap, ready to defend the city until the wall was repaired.

I am not sure if I would be a Christian today if it were not for my grandmother, she prayed for me and for the whole family consistently.

Christians often adopt this image to talk about how we can 'stand in the gap' for others; we can choose to intercede for them, to pray on their behalf, represent them to God. If your grandchildren do not know God, you can stand in the gap on their behalf, bringing their wants and needs to him as if they themselves were speaking.

The persistent widow

Then Jesus told his disciples a parable to show them that they should always pray and not give up. He said: 'In a certain town there was a judge who neither feared God nor cared what people thought. And there was a widow in that town who kept coming to him with the plea, "Grant me justice against my adversary."

'For some time he refused. But finally he said to himself, "Even though I don't fear God or care what people think, yet because this widow keeps bothering me, I will see that she gets justice, so that she won't eventually come and attack me!"'

And the Lord said, 'Listen to what the unjust judge says. And will not God bring about justice for his chosen ones, who cry out to him day and night? Will he keep putting them off? I tell you, he will see that they get justice, and quickly.'

LUKE 18:1–8

It can feel so hard to pray and pray and not see anything change. In Jesus' parable, the widow – called in some versions the 'nagging widow' – refuses to be put off by the unjust judge's refusal to hear her case.

> I suffered an eating disorder as a teenager. My grandmother prayed and prayed and supported me through those years.

Finally the judge gives in and grants her justice. For centuries Christians have used this story as an encouragement to persist in prayer. Do persist in prayer for your grandchildren, even when you can't see or tell what God is doing in response to your prayers, knowing that God, who is a just judge, will hear your cries.

Elisha

> When the servant of the man of God got up and went out early the next morning, an army with horses and chariots had surrounded the city. 'Oh no, my lord! What shall we do?' the servant asked.
>
> 'Don't be afraid,' the prophet answered. 'Those who are with us are more than those who are with them.'
>
> And Elisha prayed, 'Open his eyes, Lord, so that he may see.' Then the Lord opened the servant's eyes, and he looked and saw the hills full of horses and chariots of fire all around Elisha.
>
> 2 KINGS 6:15–17

A furious King of Aram had sent his troops to capture the prophet Elisha, and overnight they had surrounded the city of Dothan where Elisha was staying. Elisha's servant was alarmed by the sight of the army, and it wasn't until God opened his eyes that he saw the heavenly army surrounding them. If you are persisting in prayer for your grandchildren but have no idea of what God is doing, remember this story. God is busy and active even when we can't see anything at all.

Next steps: What is your experience of praying for your grandchildren? Are there times when you feel dejected or wonder if your prayers make a difference? Re-read the Bible passages above. Do any of them encourage you?

Praying for your grandchildren

There are so many ways to pray. Prayer isn't a set of regulated activities, but the opening of a heart to God, ready to share and ready to receive back the love and wisdom and comfort of an all-knowing, all-encompassing God. We have all been created differently and how we pray will differ too. Some grandparents love the discipline of daily quiet times; others pray as they go; some will drift off to sleep praying. Some have lists; others don't. Some use words; others will just have a mass of emotions and ideas and hope pouring out to God. Some will find themselves dreaming and imagining and picturing their grandchildren in their heads as they lift them to God.

The grandparents we spoke to had many different ideas for how to pray for their grandchildren, some of which you might find helpful as you and God find your own pattern of connecting and sharing your hearts. These are some of the things they told us:

- If you can, ask your grandchildren how you can pray for them and let them know that you are praying for them. Knowing that someone is praying for you is such a powerful thing for people to hear.

- Some grandparents, including some who were forbidden from talking about God with their grandchildren, described how they kept a prayer journal for each grandchild in which they recorded their thoughts and prayers, things they thought God was saying and Bible verses that stood out for that child. These will be shared with the grandchildren when they are older.

  Each grandchild has a book where we write down significant things we think God is saying – pictures, words, Bible passages. We'll give them to them when they are older, so we can say: 'Look, when you were tiny, this is what God was saying.

- A grandparent described how, when she didn't know what to pray, she just visualised bringing her grandson to Jesus, much like the parents in Mark 10:13–16, and placing him in Jesus' arms.

- In times of distress or waiting, one grandparent would light a candle and kept it burning until the situation was resolved – a way of keeping vigil, if you like, marking their intention to hold this child before God at that time.

- Several grandparents talked about praying scriptures for their grandchildren, substituting the child's name in passages such as Jeremiah 29:11; Proverbs 3:5–6; Psalm 51:10; Numbers 6:24–26; Psalm 141:3–4; Psalm 37:1–7; Matthew 6:33.

- One grandma placed photos of her grandchildren just above the kitchen sink, where she spent considerable time during the day; whenever she saw them, she used it as a prompt to pray for them.

- Pray with others. Some churches have parish grandparenting groups that meet monthly to pray for all their grandchildren. Gathering with other grandparents to share news and prayers can be so encouraging.

- Pray for your grandchildren's parents too, doing the day-to-day parenting, and sharing many of your hopes and dreams, concerns and anxieties for their children.

Next steps: How do you pray for your grandchildren? Have another look at the ideas above. Might any of these ideas be helpful? Or are there others that you might add? Pray that God will show you your next steps as you walk alongside your grandchildren: what is the one next thing I can do to help them discover who God is? Pray for God to place Christian friends and colleagues around them who can speak into their lives. Pray for yourselves, for wisdom and hope.

Do not be anxious about anything, but in every situation, by prayer and petition, with thanksgiving, present your requests to God.

PHILIPPIANS 4:6

My great-grandad prayed for his grandchildren every day, my grandad prayed for us every day, and now my dad prays for his grandchildren every day. I hope to continue that tradition if I'm ever a grandparent!

5

Giving them glimpses of God

Occasionally when I read the Bible, I spot something I've never seen before. Recently I was reading the story of the Exodus. God had told Moses that he and his brother Aaron were to go to Pharaoh and tell him to let his people, the Israelites, go:

> Afterward Moses and Aaron went to Pharaoh and said, 'This is what the Lord, the God of Israel, says: "Let my people go, so that they may hold a festival to me in the wilderness."'
> Pharaoh said, 'Who is the Lord, that I should obey him and let Israel go? I do not know the Lord and I will not let Israel go.'
> EXODUS 5:1–2

I stopped reading abruptly. I'd never noticed Pharaoh's excuse before: 'I do not know the Lord and I will not let Israel go.' That made so much sense! Pharaoh was saying, 'I don't know this god you are talking about. Why should I do what this random, possibly not even existing, god wants?'

Some of your grandchildren may be like Pharaoh, with little or no idea of who God is. When someone comes along and says, 'You can ask God', or, 'Worshipping God is a good idea', their question – conscious or unconscious – may be: I have no idea who this god is. Why on earth should I do that?

The good news is that this is where you come in. Look at what happens to Pharaoh in the next few chapters of Exodus. It takes a huge demonstration of God's power for Pharaoh to reluctantly agree to let the Israelites go. What triggers the change is that Pharaoh begins to see exactly who God is.

That's what we need to bear in mind. If someone has little or no idea of who God is, they are unlikely to take any notice of him. What they need is someone to introduce them to him so they can see why he's worth taking notice of. That's something we can all do. Whether your grandchildren need introducing to the God who longs to hold them close, or they already know him, you can let them learn from you the reality, the power and the joy of a relationship with God.

The way they had stuck to their faith through many difficult times in their lives was inspirational and contributed greatly to my belief that this is the best way to live.

Because here's the thing: Christianity isn't just a set of activities or rituals to be observed. At its heart, it's a relationship with a God who wants us to come close to him, as children, to receive everything we need: comfort, encouragement, discipline, shelter, truth and nurture. Your grandchildren might see or know about the activities you do, like prayer and worship and reading the Bible, without realising how they help you draw close to Father God and really connect with him.

Imagine how powerful it would be if your grandchildren could begin to grasp that. Right in front of their eyes they would have ideas for how they too could connect with him, draw on his strength, hear his voice, know their part in his plans and access all he has for them. They would see why a relationship with God is so wonderful.

> *My mum's parents modelled faith, love and church to me. They fostered my mum, they gave her a home and loved her when she was broken. I heard a story about how my granny sat with my mum during her worst dreams and flashbacks, and I knew this was the kind of faith I wanted to live out.*

There's a simple and natural way for you to do this. We call it 'creating windows'.

Creating windows

Near where I live is an enormous old hospital that's been converted into elegant houses and apartments. It's got a fascinating footprint; the 19th-century architects created small quadrangles and courtyards around which the wards were grouped, with pathways all the way around the perimeter. It's my favourite winter walk. Using the darkened days as an excuse, I walk my little dog all around the old hospital, tracking the ins and outs of the buildings. As I go, I naturally peek into the windows. Some are curtained; others take advantage of the seclusion to leave their curtains open, allowing me little glimpses of their lives. I see the way they have used a corner lamp to bring a certain warmth to the room. I notice a colour scheme or a particularly cosy sofa. I can see how one home's layout differs from another and decide which one I'd choose. I see the impact of a bright print on the wall and wonder if I might get one like that.

When I get these small glimpses into those homes, three things happen:

- I see the inside of the homes
- I see if there are things I'd like to do
- I get ideas for how to do the same.

Your grandchildren might see a lot of your life but never realise how deeply God is involved with it. Take how God helps you get through life's ups and downs. You might have spent your walk into town ranting to God about your colleague's rudeness yesterday. Your heart might have leapt with joy and gratitude as you realise God had answered your prayers for Sam's health. Or you invited yourself round to a Christian friend's house because you'd had an awful day and needed their wisdom and comfort. Your grandchildren probably wouldn't realise the part God had played in any of that. They might just have known you walked to town, Sam is better or that you went to your friend's house.

Much of your life with God will be hidden from your friends and family. They might not be there when you reach out to God and feel him close, or know what you and God do when you mess up. They may know you go to church, but never grasp why it's so important to you. And they are almost certainly never going to know what happens when you doubt God or question him.

When I create windows into my relationship with God for other people, three things will happen:

- They will see the inside of my relationship with God
- They will see if there are things they'd like to do
- They will get ideas for how to do the same.

> *They had objects around the house that pointed us to their faith: a prayer dice that we could roll to decide what grace to say before dinner; books that they let us look at; pictures of Jesus in my grandad's study; their church magazine that we looked through.*

Let's look at an example of how this might work. Your grandchild probably knows that you have a Bible, but they might never have read it themselves or they might think that it's just a book of old stories. By creating a window into how and why you use the Bible, you can help them see it in a whole new light.

- You can create a window into how much you value the Bible simply by reading it in front of them. If you listen to a Bible app on your phone, you could let it play while they are in the room. This gives them a glimpse that says: the Bible is important to Grandpa, and he wants to read it.

- You could mention that you're really excited to use your new Bible because it's got extra room on the pages to write notes on. This gives your grandchild a glimpse that says: Granny thinks some things in the Bible are so important she wants to write them down.

- If you mention that you want to check something you heard the preacher say to see if it agrees with what the Bible says, you create a window that says: Grandma thinks that the Bible contains God's truth.

So how do you create windows for your grandchildren?

When and how you do this will depend on all sorts of factors: what's going on in your life and your grandchildren's lives; whether you're with them or far away; how old they are. Even if they are tiny, though, creating windows is powerful. Babies and toddlers learn by watching and copying; they are tiny sponges soaking up what they see and hear, and if you create windows into your life with God, that will be going in as well.

I'm going to suggest three ways you can simply and naturally create windows in your normal interactions with your grandchildren.

Adding who God is and what he's doing into your ordinary conversations

When I'm going around my ordinary everyday life, I often think about God. From simple things, like *God must have had fun creating all those differently coloured butterflies*, to *Oh God, that's terrible news! Please be close to Harry and Belle.*

But I often don't say those things out loud, or I may even filter them out. For example, if my friend at the gym asks me what I did at the weekend, I might say I went to church on Sunday, but it's unlikely I would add, 'And God showed me something new through the sermon.' Or if I see someone fall over in the street, I might rush over to help, but only in my head be praying, 'God, help me know what to do!'

So one easy way to create windows is to add the 'God bit' into our conversations – who God was in that moment and what he was doing. Here are some ideas for how this might look like:

> *It was just everyday normal for them to talk about Jesus or answered prayer or stories of things they'd done with him, and how he saved them.*

- Say you bump into a friend who's only too happy to give you a lift to the hospital next week. You could just say, 'Jackie's going to give me a lift', or you could add, 'I was so worried, I've been asking God how I could get there so early and look, he sent Jackie!' This simple addition gives your grandchild a glimpse into how you depend on God and what he does.

- You've got your favourite worship music playing in the car when you pick up your grandchildren from school. Why not add, 'This song really helps me understand who God is', or, 'This song helps me feel close to God – I love singing it at the moment.'

- It can work for the tougher bits of life too. Imagine you've had a health scare and your family anxiously calls you. Just by saying, 'I had a fright when my blood pressure hit the roof yesterday; the staff at the A&E were so kind, and I was so aware of God being there too,' you create a window into how God makes a difference for you.

That's all. Just add in the God bit that's probably already in your head. This instantly creates a window into the impact God has on us, showing your family that God is real and makes a difference – and that he could do that for them too.

Next steps: Take a moment to think about the last time you were with your grandchildren. Were there moments you had with God, but your grandchildren wouldn't have known? Have a think about windows you might create for them next time.

Do what you do with God in front of them

We learn so much just by being shown what something looks like. I coach junior netball and spend an inordinate amount of time each week trying to teach girls to play well. Over the years I've discovered that sometimes words aren't enough. 'Turn on your right foot, face forwards and pass the ball' is confusing for many. Which is my right foot? Which way is forwards – the way I was facing or the new way? And pass it to who? But what really works is to clearly model the movement. So I do it in front of them.

This modelling is so helpful for the girls watching. They don't just hear what to do; they see it. That doesn't mean they instantly become brilliant at the move. Sometimes the penny drops immediately, but more often, as they see the move repeated over time, they begin to understand it and can do it themselves.

You can use the same idea to help grandchildren get a glimpse of how to relate to God themselves. When you do what you normally do with God in front of them, you model for them how

> *I observed her praying, going to church without fail each week, praying before a meal, at night. She lived the life rather than preached it to me.*

your relationship with God works – and then if they want to, they can copy that. What you do depends on your circumstances, your grandchildren and how you relate to God, but here are some examples:

- From time to time, pray out loud when it's not bedtime or mealtime – just because that's what you're doing in your head. 'Father God, which jumper would James like?' might not sound like a model prayer, but for your curious grandchild it creates a window into the fact that you pray about everything. 'Jesus, keep us safe as we journey today' gives grandchildren a glimpse into how you rely on God's protection.

- If something from this week's sermon or your Bible reading notes has struck home, you might mention it in front of your grandchild: 'This verse from Psalm 23 is such a comfort to me at the moment – I'm going to write it out and stick it on my mirror so that I see it every morning!'

- If it's appropriate, invite them to do 'God things' alongside you, so they get to experience it and have a go themselves. This could be letting them accompany you to evensong at church, giving them a picture Bible to sit and look at as you grab five minutes to catch up with your Bible, or getting them to help you set up for the small group that's meeting later in your home. It could even be sending an older grandchild a copy of the same book you're reading and then discussing what you both think when you call them later.

Next steps: Think about what you normally do with God, particularly when you're not in church. How is he involved in your decision-making and your routines? Are there windows you could create into any of that for your grandchildren?

Harness the power of telling stories

When I worked at my local church, I had the bright idea of starting a Monday morning small group for mums with

young children. The idea was that after the school drop-off
they would head over to church for pastries and coffee, and
study the Bible together.

After a few months, one of our older ladies, a stalwart of
the church, approached me. 'Monday mornings would
work really well for me,' she said. 'Can I join your group?'
Rather reluctantly, I said yes, and Jenny joined the mums.
Soon, other older ladies got wind of this and turned up too.
At first I was a little annoyed. This was my mums' group! It
wouldn't be the same if all these old ladies turned up! I was
right. It wasn't the same. It was better.

What I quickly learned was that these old ladies were perfectly positioned to disciple the young mums. Their long
lives had taught them so much about God. They knew what
it was like to watch a teenager drift away from God. They'd
nursed relatives through long and painful illnesses. They'd
had times when they doubted and questioned. They'd seen
God answer prayer wonderfully and learned what happened
when they couldn't hear him. They'd fostered children who'd
been through terrible trauma. These ladies had been there,
done that and got the T-shirt, multiple times. The stories
they told were powerful and revealed so much about who
God is, and I – and the young mums – lapped them up.

Just because you have lived a long time, you have so many
stories to tell and to share. Grandchildren love stories, particularly stories about their families. I loved hearing from my
grandma how she'd left her eleven siblings on Tyneside to
go down to London to become a nursemaid, and later what

it was like to be evacuated with my four-year-old mum as the blitz started. I was fascinated when my other grandma described being a flapper in the 1920s! None of my grand-parents were Christians, so they didn't talk about God. But as you share stories of your life with your grandchildren, you can create powerful windows into who God is.

There are other stories that are powerful too. The stories of your everyday life show grandchildren that God is busy and active in the little as well as the big things. I remember my mother, a teacher, talking about a little girl in her class who was so difficult to like, and how she'd resolved to pray daily for her. It was such an eye-opener for me in how to deal with hard relation-ships. And finally, don't forget the great stories of the heroes of our faith. I grew up on stories of Brother Andrew, Gladys Aylward and C.T. Studd, and later eagerly read the stories of Nicky Cruz and Jackie Pullinger, ordinary people who risked every-thing to partner with God.

A story that my grand-parents told of God's provision for them during the Depression stayed with me. As a young parent I was faced with a similar economic crisis. I was able to bring it to God because I knew he had met my grandparents' need and would then meet mine!

Let's look at what those stories might look like.

- **Stories of your life:** how God helped you in decisions; who he was in difficult times; where, looking back, you can see his guidance and direction. For example: 'We didn't know which house to choose when we moved to Leeds, and then God...'; 'When your nanna was dying, I was so angry with God, but then...'

- **Stories of your everyday:** the little interactions you and God have might feel so mundane to you, but to others, those stories speak of a God who's interested and involved in every aspect of our lives. For example: 'When I was queuing at the pharmacy, God moved my heart to pray for this lady in the line ahead of me...'; 'I was really fed up at work today, but God reminded me...'

- **Stories of other people:** share the snippets of who God has been for friends at church or stories you might have heard on Christian radio or in the news. 'Look at how that person chose to forgive her daughter's murderers' is so powerful, but so is: 'Andy was telling me that he's no idea what to do now he's been made redundant, but he's so sure God has a plan he doesn't seem worried at all!'

- **Stories your grandchild may need to hear:** stories can be particularly helpful when your grandchild is facing something new or has questions about God. Sharing how God helped you find your spouse, or what happened when you failed an exam, or how lost you felt when you left home can create important windows for a grandchild who is facing the same thing.

- **Stories of heroes of the faith:** there are books available to suit all ages, from toddlers to teens; you could give them as presents, or have them lying around to share; or you could watch or suggest film or video versions of the stories.

Be confident to share all sorts of stories: not just stories of when God showed up, but stories of the ups and downs – when you doubted or weren't sure what God was doing; stories of the tiny and stories of the huge. As you tell stories, you are shaping your grandchildren's views of the world, showing them how God is busy, active and faithful. Stories will show them what's possible and what's true and help them hang on to truth in a world that's shouting loudly.

Next steps: Do you already share stories with your grandchildren? How could you create opportunities to do this? Think about your life with God. What stories might your grandchildren like to hear? Think about each of your grandchildren. Would you be able to share stories of faith with them? How could you do this best?

But what if I can't?

It might not always feel simple or right to create windows into your life with God. You might have been told you can't talk about God with your grandchildren, or you may feel uncomfortable doing so because of your family's beliefs or dynamics. In that situation, you might feel that deliberately creating windows into your faith would be disrespectful or even underhanded.

The good news is that you will create windows into your life with God just by being you. Imagine you spent time with a family who loved musical theatre. You'd hear them practising the songs from their latest show. You'd watch them say they can't come to the pub because it's rehearsals and they don't want to miss one. You'd see the pleasure opening night brings them or watch as they spend hours building the set. You might not become an avid musical theatre fan, but just being with them will open your eyes to how much fun some people find it and how it impacts them. Just being around them will give you information about musical theatre and how you could get involved if you wanted to. In the same way, just being yourself with God in front of your grandchildren will speak volumes to them about who God is and give them information about how they can get to know him.

On the cupboard in the kitchen they had a prayer list of people to pray for on different days, and I remember seeing my name on the list as a child and being struck that someone was praying for me regularly.

Others might worry about letting their grandchildren see the inside of their rather imperfect faith. Surely we don't want them to know about the periods of doubt, when we disobeyed or God just didn't seem to show up?

Perhaps surprisingly, there's enormous power in sharing those times too. If you were only to create windows into the good times, how will your grandchildren know how to relate to God when they are furious with him or have got things wrong or are in pain or struggling? They need to know what a relationship with God is like then, because they will have times like that too. They need to see glimpses of a faith that works in the messy bits of life so that when they mess up or are confused or broken, they know what they can do.

Keep it simple

Let's go back to my netball analogy. During matches, the girls can sometimes make what's essentially a very simple task – passing the ball safely from one end of the court to the other – very complicated. I often find myself shouting to my team from the sideline: 'Keep it simple! Just do what's in front of you!'

I'd say the same about creating windows. We really want people to 'get' God, to understand his beauty and majesty and compassion, and so it can be tempting to grab every opportunity and turn it into a 'teachable moment'. But the joy of creating windows is that it's just a window. Just a way for your grandchildren to glimpse you and God doing life together. Sometimes you might feel it's right to explain something or your grandchild might ask you questions, but that's an added bonus. You don't need to tell them everything or create windows into things you're not ready to share or aren't appropriate for them. Very often, no words are needed – giving a lonely person a hug or letting them see you giving up a night in to volunteer with Street Pastors can speak volumes.

Remember the poppies. Creating windows is just another way to drop another splash of colour on to the canvas; a way to gradually help your grandchildren build up a big picture of who God is and what he does.

6

Making sense of life

I grew up in church and loved Jesus. Aged six, I made a commitment to follow him for the rest of my life. I had a relationship with God that I treasured. I prayed, read my Bible and enjoyed church. I went to Sunday school and knew all the answers. I'd devoured the children's stories of classic missionaries that graced our bookshelves. I tried my very best to be a good Christian. Then, one of the elders in our church fell gravely sick. We were all praying hard and hoping that he would get better. But my nine-year-old heart was confused and questioning. 'Why?' I asked my dad. 'Why don't you and the other elders just anoint him with oil like it says here in James chapter 5? Then he'll be healed!' My father sadly shrugged and didn't answer. When Harry died a few weeks later, I was left with big questions about faith and healing and the truth of the Bible.

As parents, carers and grandparents, we are made to help kids understand the world. We explain everything! If you hit someone, they will get angry. Wait at the crossing until the signal is green, then it's safe to cross. Exams are stressful and this is how to revise. Now you've started dating, these are some things you need to think about. This is why voting's important, and this is why I'd choose that party. We help them understand everything, from the little to the big: from watch out for the dog poo on the grass to how to cope when your parents divorce or a friend dies. We give them a framework for life.

Children also need a spiritual framework. Rachel Turner, in *Parenting Children for a Life of Faith*, says:

> We live in a hurt, broken and beautiful world in relationship with an entirely real and active God. Our children need help in understanding the world with God in it, and working out how to engage with him in response.[17]

As I went through my teen years, the gulf between what I was experiencing and what I thought the Bible said grew bigger and bigger. I believed that sex outside marriage was bad, but no one had told me how to navigate the feelings I had. What does 'God loves me' mean when my parents are arguing? I knew God created the world in six days, but then I learned about fossils and evolution and that all seemed to make so much sense. I had questions, but very few answers.

Looking back, I can see why, as soon as I left home, I stopped going to church. It was nothing to do with rebellion; I actually liked church. It was simpler than that. It was that I'd stopped seeing that God was relevant. I had a big bundle of truth about God – he loves me, he protects me, he wants good things for me, he's always there, and so much more – but no idea how any of that fit into my real life.

As I've grown older, I've begun to join up some of the dots about who God is in my life. I've also learned that sometimes it's okay not to know all the answers. As I process what I'm seeing, whether that's another war atrocity, a friend's illness or even just the bumps of my everyday life, I can draw on a bank of information and experiences that help me make sense of things and keep me grounded in God when life sucks or just doesn't seem to make sense.

Your grandchildren need that too. They need a framework for life that includes God, because it's only when we have that framework that the world truly makes sense. One of the wonderful privileges of having a voice in the life of a child or young person is that you can help them begin to make sense of the world with God in it, just like you help them make sense of their everyday world.

> *My grandmother used to write me letters and tell me of her experiences of Jesus' faithfulness and her prayer through difficult times when I was in my late teens and when I had just left home. These were some of the most significant things she ever shared with me.*

At this point, you might be thinking *Gosh, I have no idea how I can do that!* Maybe you're not used to explaining who God is or feel you don't know him very well yourself. But there's good news. We don't need to be Bible scholars or theologians to help children understand who God is in their everyday lives. They simply need a guide: someone just a little bit further down the road who has experienced similar things or wrestled with similar questions.

Framing

Parenting for Faith's key tool of framing is a way to help kids build up a foundation of truth about who God is in the world and in their individual lives, so he makes sense to them.

Framing is simply drawing your grandchildren's attention to what they are looking at and helping them understand it. Imagine you are taking your grandchildren for a walk. As you go, you might point out a spiky little insect and wonder at it together. You'll warn them about the muddy puddle coming up ahead or share a story about what happened when you got your trousers snagged on that bit of barbed wire. You simply help them understand the journey.

And that's all framing is: helping them understand the journey they are on and where God fits into it. Just as you naturally frame life for them – from the running commentary you give to your eight-week-old grandson as you push him through the park to answering life's big questions with your 18-year-old – you can frame life with God for them at all ages and stages. Whether your grandchildren are sold-out Christians, convinced atheists or just totally uninterested; whether they are tiny or 20, you can help them understand the world with God in it.

> I remember, the first time I won money in a competition, Grandma explaining about tithing and encouraging me to give ten percent back to God.

We are going to look at four straightforward ways to frame things for your grandchildren:

- explain everything
- answer their questions
- jumpstart conversations about God
- lay foundations for their future.

Explain everything

The first way to frame is to explain who God is in their ordinary everyday bits of life.

As you go about your day, you probably have an idea about what God is doing or who he is: as you try to make a decision about your elderly mother's care, you pray for God's guidance; when the bus arrives just before the rain starts to pour, you thank God for his timing.

Your grandchildren might not have any idea that God is involved in people's everyday lives. If you can help them understand that, then you are immediately painting a new picture of God for them: a God who is relevant, interested and active – and who could be part of their lives too.

This applies to the small things as well as the big. Take the recycling, for example. For some reason, every time I trudge out to put the glass in its special box and to separate the plastics from the paper, I remember God's command to us in Genesis to take care of the world. We can frame that simply and naturally, just by adding the 'God bit' to our normal conversations: 'Hand me the recycling box please. It's funny, but every time I do this, I remember God asked us specially to take care of his world, and this is an important way I can do that.' Wham! With just one sentence, you've framed for your grandchild that God cares about the world, and he wants us to partner with him in doing that.

As you explain gently that a family member is really quite poorly, you could add what's going on in your head: 'I'm scared too, and when I'm scared the first thing I do is to tell God that. It seems to settle me down, like now I've told him he's got my back.' When your three-year-old grandson falls over and scrapes his knee, as you find the first aid kit and wipe away their tears, you can also add the God-truths you have in your head: 'Poor Joel! Come here and let me help. Let's ask God to take the pain away.'

> My grandpa particularly talked about our role in caring for creation... This was so important to him and is now important to me. He also talked to me about heaven and how much he wanted to go there when he was poorly. He prayed every night that he could go see Jesus and so we were able to rejoice when he died that he was with his Saviour. That had a huge impact on me.

You can also explain things to them by adding in the 'whys' as well as the 'whats'. So often we talk about things without explaining what they have to do with God. By explaining the 'why' as well as the 'what', you can help your grandchildren connect the activity with who God is.

For example:

- Imagine your 13-year-old granddaughter has fallen out with her best friend. You might say to her, 'Aisha, have you prayed about it?' But how powerful to then add the 'why': 'Aisha, have you prayed about it? Because then you've invited God into the problem and made space for him to talk to you.' In just one sentence, you've explained that prayer is more than just a one-way conversation and that God wants to be part of even the messy bits of life.

- As you pick up the Bible storybook to read to four-year-old Angus, you can simply frame it for him: 'I love reading stories from the Bible with you because they are stories God's given us.' Angus now knows that these aren't just stories – they are stories from God.

- As your granddaughter breathes a sigh of relief that you've finally left church, you could say: 'Thank you for being patient while I chatted to Glenys. I wanted to make time for her because she's lonely and God wants us to look out for lonely people.' By framing why you spent so much time with Glenys, you've explained to your granddaughter that God cares for lonely people and he wants us to help.

Explaining the part God played in your decision-making is also a powerful way to frame. You might be telling your six-year-old grandchild the story of why you bought your new house. Adding in the 'why' – that as soon as you walked through the door, you felt God say, 'This is the one' – frames so many things: that God cares about even which house you live in, that he speaks to us and that you do what he says!

Every time you frame, you're building a picture of who God is in the world, that will help your grandchildren see not just God's relevance, but his goodness too.

Next steps: Think about the last time you saw your grand-children or chatted to them. What did you talk about or do together? Can you see things you framed for them, or could have framed for them – ways to help them see who God is or what he was doing?

Answer their questions

As well as laying a general foundation about who God is, you may also find that your grandchildren have questions about God. And some of them can be crackers! 'Why did God make slugs?' ranks as one of

> *I was able to ask questions about faith… I can remember asking my grandad questions like did the snake only talk in the creation story.*

my favourites (and I still don't know the answer). You may also be asked for help with ethical dilemmas or be asked huge questions, about death, miracles, sex and more – and that is wonderful, because when a child or a teen is asking questions, it's because they are trying to make sense of who God is. Is he real? Does he care? Have Christians understood him properly? What does he really want? Questions are a wonderful opportunity to help grandchildren understand God, and it's so important that we answer them.

At this point, you might feel ready to duck out of this completely. We often get nervous about answering kids' spiritual questions. What if we don't give the right answer, or put them off God? Most of us would say we don't know enough theology or have the skills to be able to answer every question a grandchild has.

That's fine. Framing isn't about having the right answer. It's about creating a culture where it's okay to ask big questions about God. It's about modelling how we can explore and wonder together, and sharing how we answer those questions, and what we do when we just don't know.

At Parenting for Faith we have a simple four-step process that will help grandparents and children answer pretty much any question well – and more importantly frame that God is real, relevant and interested.

Whatever the question, we can use these four steps:

1 **What do you think?** Children and teens ask questions for all sorts of reasons. It may be hypothetical. They may be testing out something someone's told them at school. Or it may be something that's troubling them personally. By starting with this question, it helps you understand what's in their hearts and minds.

2 **What do we know?** Chat together about what you already know – according to the Bible, your own experience and wise people around you – that will help you answer the question.

3 **What do we not know?** There are lots of things that we don't know about scripture and theology and about God. As you talk, be open about that fact. This models that it's okay to not know everything and that not everything has a simple answer.

4 **Share how you handle the question yourself.** Help frame for them how you've handled this question in your own life. This is such a powerful step, because what kids need to know *more* than a right answer is how to handle the tough stuff or doubts that come up in life. If you can give them a window into how you've processed the question, they can start to figure out how they will too.

And then together you can decide your next steps, which might be:

• we're happy with the answer we've come up with
• we'll have a chat with God or a wise person
• let's do a bit of research and see what we think then.

Let's have a look at how this might work. Say your eight-year-old grandson bounces into the room and asks: 'Does God have ears?'

1 What do you think?

'Gosh, that's an interesting question? What do you think?'

'Well, Robbie says he couldn't because he's not got a body like us, but Mum says God listens to us so maybe he does?'

2 What do we know?

'You're right, the Bible does say that God listens to us. I know that God hears me, because sometimes he answers, but I'm not sure if he listens with ears or another way. Genesis tells us that people are made in the image of God, so we must be like him in some ways at least.'

3 What do we not know?

'Well, I'm not sure what God's body is like. And I don't know whether when the Bible says we're made in God's image it means our hearts and minds are like his or we have the same sort of body.'

4 Share how you handle the question yourself.

'Hmm, that is such a good question! I'm not sure if he has ears or not. But you know what? I don't really mind if he has or hasn't, because I do know that somehow, he can listen to me and he cares about what I say and that sometimes I can hear his answer back.'

Please don't think that you have to answer questions if you don't feel confident or knowledgeable enough. But do explain that to your grandchild. It's fine to say: 'My goodness, what a question! I'm really not sure. I know that Christians really disagree on this. Is it okay if I don't answer it yet? I'll go and have a chat with Paul at church – and when you're next round we can chat some more.' Just by explaining that, you are showing that Christians don't have to have all the answers; it's normal not to know, but it's good to try to work out the answers the best way you can.

If you do feel confident or that it's appropriate, you might want to wade into questions that touch on tricky subjects. As you do so, you can share how you arrived at the view you did or that you're still making up your mind. You can point to people, places or resources which might be helpful. You could share how you've wrestled with God about this, or still find those bits which talk about it in the Bible tricky, so this is where you've landed up. If you later change your mind about an answer you've given, go back and share that with your grandchild. 'You know we were talking about if God made the world in exactly six days or not? Well, I was listening to this podcast and they said…'

Jumpstart conversations about God

It doesn't always feel simple to start chatting about God, particularly if your grandchildren don't ask questions about him or don't know much about him. By harnessing their natural curiosity, however, you can jumpstart natural conversations which will give you space to help share God with them. The trick is to ask questions about God that have no right answer, particularly if they aren't the sort of questions people expect about God!

For example, as you're looking out at a starry night, you could just ask: 'I wonder what God does at night?' Your conversation with your grandchild might wander all over the place: from the idea of God never sleeping, to whether he watches each of us individually, to whether he can see Australia and Scotland at the same time.

You might ask: 'I wonder who Jesus hung out with at school?'; 'Has God ever asked you to do anything?'; 'What does God do when we pray?'; or 'If you could add one person from the Bible to your household, who would you pick and why?' Enjoy the conversations and see where they lead.

On our website, we have a free download to help you get started: 'Questions to ask your kid to spark an interesting conversation…' (**parentingforfaith.org/101-questions**).

Next steps: Do your grandchildren ask you questions about God? You may want to practise the four steps or even explain to them you've discovered this great way to tackle any question about God, and ask if they have one for you to try!

If your grandchildren don't talk about God, could you use questions to jumpstart conversations about him? What sort of questions would work for them or for your family situation?

Lay foundations for their future

The fourth way we're thinking about framing is how to lay good God foundations for your grandchildren's future.

As grandparents, you watch your grandchildren grow and change. You'll be able to spot much of what's next for them, not just the obvious next step of nursery or high school, but also things like the almost inevitable ending of a first love or the fact that in a year your anxious 17-year-old will be leaving school and needing a job. You might be aware, perhaps long before your grandchildren are, of the increasing tension between their parents.

You can use the key tool of framing to help prepare grandchildren for things that are coming up in their lives. Such an important part of grandparenting is to be another safe person for your grandchildren, to support them and their parents both practically and with wisdom and care. And you can also help them see who God is and who he wants to be in any situation they are facing.

> I used to eat breakfast in bed with my grandma and I would tell her about what was going on in my life, and she'd use my experiences to tell me about a Bible story, or Jesus going through something similar, and how prayer or scripture could help me.

When I'm facing something new or scary, I automatically draw on what I already know about God to help me. If I'm running low on money, worried about the bills or how I'll pay for the holiday, I might remember times when God has provided for me or recall stories of how he dramatically stepped in to plug the gap for others. If I've been humiliated, I remember the story of Hagar, powerless and ill-treated, yet finding hope in God, or remember that however tempted I am to retaliate, God will help me resist that temptation. By sharing those experiences and that knowledge with grandchildren, you help to lay foundations of truth for them to draw on in the future.

So if your grandson is facing important exams in the summer, stressed from a continual stream of mock exams and worried about getting into sixth form, alongside the conversations of how he is feeling and how you can help, you might say: 'I remember when I did my exams, I was so worried about failing them. I thought I'd be a nobody. But what made a difference was I realised that none of God's heroes in the Bible were there because they were smart. Moses had a stammer, Jonah ran away – and I realised that my exam results weren't the be all and end all for God. I'd be okay even if I did fail.'

You can reassure your granddaughters that they'll be okay when they move to the other side of the country: 'I know it's a long way away and you don't know anyone. That must feel really hard at the moment. When we moved, I felt so lonely. But I knew that the Bible says God sets the lonely in families, so I started looking out for the friends God was sending me. And I found them!'

Next steps: Think about each of your grandchildren. Is there anything coming up in their lives where they might need help to see where God is? What experiences have you and God gone through together that might help them? Have a chat with God about how you might frame it for them.

Framing for all ages and stages

It might be hard to imagine what framing actually looks like for a newborn who barely opens their eyes, or for the angry teen who doesn't have time for anyone's advice. Or perhaps you have a grandchild with cognitive needs, or a grandchild who barely ever stops moving long enough to listen to you. It can help to remember that framing is simply helping them know what they are looking at.

While framing for a baby may feel a little awkward, it's no different from the framing you do for them all the time as you chatter away about life: 'Oh, we'd better hurry or we'll miss the bus!' or 'Apple's good for your tummy, yum yum.' It's a simple next step just to add God into your explanations: 'God made those lovely apples. Thank you, God!' While tucking them into the cot, as you say 'Sleep tight', you can add 'God's here with you.' Those simple comments help establish an awareness of God as part of their everyday life right from the beginning.

It may feel hard to frame who God is for children who are struggling. Maybe they have experienced trauma, or find it hard to understand the world like other children. It can be helpful to remember that your love and empathy speak about who God is; cuddling a sad child or listening to their woes is powerful and important, as it communicates that you are there for them and that you love them and are connected to them. And then, when it feels right, you can add stories of who God was when you experienced loss or confusion or whatever it is. Frame what they are looking at and what you think they need next. Be their guide as they face the next steps on their journey.

Some children really aren't interested in God. They may never have realised he has something to say to them, or even that he's real. Others may be super busy, never sitting still or even questioning life. Some children or teens may be done with God, or not interested in anyone's advice. Framing still works for those kids. If you have any of those in your life, simply by adding bits of

My Opa had an incredible testimony of life in prison camp as a young boy in Indonesia. I always felt safe, intrigued, inspired about his life and his story.

framing here and there or engaging them in an interesting conversation, you are highlighting to them that for you, God is real, active and involved in all our lives and giving them a pool of truth, wisdom and stories about God and people that will be available whenever they need it.

And finally

You don't need to feel the pressure to frame everything for your grandchildren. Just frame what comes naturally to you. It will soon become second nature. And as you get used to the ideas in this chapter, chat with God about what he might want you to do next.

Remember the poppies. One splash at a time.

7

Getting to grips with God

I remember as a young child being taken to visit my great-grandmother. I'd never met her before, but I'd seen pictures from the 1930s of this rather stern-looking matriarch and I'd heard my father's stories of how she'd kept him and his brother in line when they stayed with her as children. I felt more and more nervous as we drew closer and closer to Sheffield, and as we stood outside her flat waiting for the door to open, I tried to hide behind my parents. I didn't want anything to do with this scary person! My view of Nanna changed very quickly, though, as she revealed the plates of cake and cream buns she'd prepared to welcome her family.

You might have noticed that children can have quite distinct views about people. Babies can be suddenly shy in the presence of a stranger, even if that stranger loves them dearly. Kids come home from primary school with tales about how unfair their teacher is. Teenagers are clearly looking for an opportunity to dive out of the room when distant relatives come to visit, anticipating the boredom to come.

If we don't know someone very well or we have some wrong ideas about them, it affects our relationship with them. Like the baby, we might be suspicious about them; like the eight-year-old, we might have formed very strong – but incorrect – opinions about who they are; or like the teen, we might try to avoid them altogether.

My view of who God is has been formed over time. I'm sure yours has, too. You've heard sermons, read the Bible and heard wise people speak. You'll be able to recall times when you prayed and felt God answer, or when you were in distress and knew his comfort, or when you needed guidance and God gave you that. We're all on a journey of getting to know God better and better, and your grandchildren are on that journey too. Some might know him well; others may not have received much information about him at all – but they will all be forming views about him.

Children and young people get their ideas about God from many different places. Some will hear about him at church or through their Bibles, but they will also be exposed to many other ideas about him, some helpful and others less so. They'll be hearing opinions and stories from RE teachers, friends and their parents. There will be snippets of ideas in movies, books, social media, podcasts and videos. Their own experiences, good and bad, might also be shaping how they think about God. From their earliest years, children are forming views about who God is and, as they do so, they can end up with ideas about God that are distorted and affect how, or even if, they want to relate to him. If we don't like someone or think they are weird, we might be reluctant to spend time with them – and it can be the same with God.

One of the things children and young people need is to form a healthy understanding of God, and the best people to help them do that are the people God has placed around them.

In this chapter we're going to explore two ideas for helping grandchildren build a healthy picture of God: giving them a broad and balanced view of who he is, and gently unwinding any distorted ideas they have about him.

Building a broad and balanced view

I wonder if you, like me, suffer from incorrigible nosiness when you pass a building site. Near where I live there's a new development of houses that I've been told are going to be next level in terms of comfort and energy efficiency, delivering a new standard of town-centre living. So naturally, my curiosity was aroused. What would they look like? How big will they be? Could I imagine myself living there one day? Inevitably, I found myself walking towards the site, only to be faced with enormous blue panels shutting the site off from public view. Frustrated, I scouted round and then I saw it. The gap. I pressed my eye up to it and looked through – and saw a strip of mud, a few bricks and the end of a silent concrete mixer. My view was so narrow it told me almost nothing and certainly didn't help me decide if this was a place I would like to live.

In the same way, if someone has a narrow view of God, knowing just a little about him, they may struggle to relate to him or understand who he is.

God has so many aspects to his character. We know about him from our own experiences – maybe the way we felt his peace when we were in distress, or believe that he heard our prayers. We have heard stories from others or in the Bible that tell us more. We learn even more about him from the many names there are for him: shepherd, provider, most high, our peace, redeemer, judge, and the list goes on.[18] Over the years we gradually built up a broader and broader picture of God.

Because they haven't had so much experience of life, your grandchildren are unlikely to have such a broad view of God. There are some simple things you can do to help broaden their view so that they understand him better.

> My paternal grandmother had a poster on bathroom wall that said something like: 'I believe in the sun even when it does not shine; I believe in love even when I don't feel it; I believe in God even when he is silent.' I remember as young child asking about it and her telling me how God was always with us even in difficult times and I knew she had lived through some difficult times. That stuck with me.

1 **Be aware of your own bias.** Most of us tend to have favourite aspects of God's character. When I was a children's worker, I loved telling the big dramatic stories like Daniel in the lions' den or the Exodus, which

highlighted God's power and righteousness. After a while I realised that although these were great stories, there were other sorts of stories the children needed to hear: how God met Elijah as a 'gentle whisper'; how Ruth's quiet faithfulness was so important for God's plans; how because Mary sat at Jesus' feet she was able to learn from him.[19] These aren't dramatic stories, but they contain important, different truths about God. It can be useful to spend a few minutes thinking about the aspects of God's character you are drawn to in case it is unconsciously affecting how you talk about God or share who he is with your grandchildren, or even the stories of God you share with them.

2 **Deliberately add balance.** As you talk about God, you can deliberately comment on aspects of his character, particularly if you think this might be something your grandchildren might not be aware of.

   a For younger children, a useful tool is to talk about 'When I… God is'. For example, 'When I am sad, God draws close to me,' or, 'When I mess up, God still loves me.'

   b With older children, you might want to talk about who God was at different times in your life: when you needed guidance, when you were scared, when you got things wrong, when you were celebrating.

   c You can also talk about the names of God and how each one tells a different story about God. God 'the

Alpha and the Omega' talks about a different side of God than 'God who sees me'; 'Lord of the angel armies' paints a different picture of God than 'the Lord, who heals you'. But all of them are aspects of the same God.[20]

3 **Dig into Bible stories.** If you are able to share the Bible with your grandchildren, you can have fascinating conversations that will help them explore more about him. You can point out how patient God was with Gideon and wonder if he's ever been that patient with you. You can share the beautiful picture in Zephaniah of God singing over us and ask your grandchild if they think God still does that today. You can wonder about why God sent Jonah to help the Ninevites change, even though they were his enemies.[21]

> *My husband finds it easy to talk about faith, but I don't. So I use Christian books to help share big ideas and trigger good conversations.*

4 **Ask questions about God with no right answers.** Questions such as 'I wonder what makes God sad?' or 'How is God different to Father Christmas?' give children permission to wonder about God and dig deeper into his character. We have a free download of 'Questions to ask your kid to spark an interesting conversation...' on our website (**parentingforfaith.org/101-questions**) that can get you started on a fascinating journey of wondering and learning together.

Next steps: Take a few moments to think about your own picture of God. How was it formed? Then think about your grandchildren. Who and what is helping them form their views of God? Which of the four ideas above could you use to help broaden that view?

Unwind distorted views of God that you spot

 I'm sure if my parents had realised that I was frightened of Nanna because I had formed a skewed view of her, they would have immediately helped me reshape that view. They might have shared stories of her kindness or explained that she had disciplined my father and uncle to help them learn to stay safe on a busy road. In a similar way, we all get mixed up about God from time to time, and may need help unwinding any misunderstandings.

As your grandchildren grow older, you might notice that they have a view of God that doesn't sit quite right with you. Below, we're going to touch on some common wrong views of God that children and teens sometimes have, and explore how, if you spot any of these, you can gently shepherd your grandchildren's views to nudge them in the right direction.

This can feel daunting, but it's no different from if they were talking about your neighbour George. Your grandson may only have seen him twice and both times George was rushing to catch the bus and dashed past you both on the stairs. 'Grandad, your neighbour's really rude,' your grandson might say. 'He never stops to say hello!' Knowing that George isn't rude at all, you would naturally try to unwind this view. You might tell your grandson a story of George's chattiness, or how he came round and stayed all day when you were worried about leaving the cat when you had a hospital appointment. If you spot a wrong idea about God, you simply do the same: you share what you do know about God. It's a bit like those old-fashioned balance scales: if there's a wrong view of God on one side, you can help to balance the scales by adding truth about God on the other.

Distant God

Some children – and some adults – might have a view of God that he is far away; too far away to take notice of them. They may be seeing pictures of God, high up in his heavenly home, directing operations from afar, or assume that the God of the universe must be busy sorting out countries and disasters and that little people don't count.

Children or teens who have this view of God may feel that they aren't important enough, or that their situations are not grave enough, to warrant his attention. They may feel that God has too many other important things to do, and they don't want to impose their little needs on him and distract him from his main jobs. Children who believe that God is distant may be reluctant to pray or assume he isn't interested in ordinary day-to-day things.

If you suspect your grandchild has this view of God, you could create windows into times you've known God to be close to you or share stories of times he's worked in the ordinary bits of your life. Or you could share scriptures such as Matthew 10:29–30, where Jesus tells us that God cares even for the sparrows and knows exactly how many hairs we have on our heads. Pointing out where God is close gives your grandchild different information about God which will help unwind their view.

Angry God

Another common wrong view of God is that he's angry. Cartoon Gods look down from heaven, a flash of lightning erupting from their fingers as they smite sinners. Children learn about sin; they might read about how God will judge everyone one day, or hear Bible stories like

> *When I thought I had done something unforgivable, my grandpa listened to how I was feeling and why I was so worried and then shared how God forgives and that I didn't need to be afraid. That was around 35 years ago, but I can still picture the scene and how releasing it was to feel forgiven.*

Adam and Eve being sent out of Eden or the city of Jericho being destroyed, and worry that they are in the line for punishment. They hear that God is watching us all the time and conclude that he's waiting to pounce on us when we get it wrong.

Children or teens with this view may be fearful of God or be overly focused on not letting God down. They may be reluctant to draw close to God in case he spots them and sees that they have got things wrong.

Again, to rebalance this view, you might want to talk about times when you've got things wrong and how you had to come to God for forgiveness. Sharing the difference it made can help children and teens understand that when God sees sin, he longs to gather the sinner in his arms and help set things right. You could point to Bible stories like the prodigal son or characters like David or Jonah, both of whom sinned greatly, but whom God continued to love, forgive and restore, despite their ups and downs. You might want to frame how you understand God as both our judge and our loving Father.

Unpredictable God

God can seem very mysterious. Why does he heal some people and not others? Why doesn't he rescue the perse-cuted? Does he hear my prayers? Some children may have experienced situations where they desperately wanted God to show up but he didn't. We sometimes use phrases such as 'God works in mysterious ways' or 'It will all work out for good in the end', which really don't help anyone understand what God's doing at all. If you find God unpredictable you may feel that you can't understand God and you definitely can't count on him when you need him.

Children and teens with this view of God might be reluctant to invest in a relationship with him, because they don't think he's reliable. They might have lots of questions about why God allows this, or doesn't do that, or they might just try to avoid him altogether.

It can be powerful to allow your grandchildren to see that it's normal to have questions and even doubts about God. Telling stories of times you've doubted God or not been able to understand him creates a window into the normal ups and downs of faith, which can be reassuring to someone who's feeling a bit wobbly about God. You might look at some stories from the Bible where God wasn't predictable and wonder together, for example, how John the Baptist might have felt when he was arrested or what Daniel would have felt as he was left alone, trapped in the lions' den.

You can also unwind this view of God by talking about how you cope with those moments when you don't understand what God's doing. When I'm in that place, I've learned to go back to what I do know about God. Your neighbour George seems rude when he rushes past you on the stairs, but you would also know that yesterday you had a great catch-up over a cup of tea, or you saw him helping your other neighbour with a heavy package, or you remember how kind he was when your wife died. His behaviour in that moment might seem rude, but you have a whole wealth of other knowledge about him that tells you otherwise.

In the same way, you can point your grandchild to other truths you know about God that help you when you aren't sure who God is or what he is doing; for example, that you still don't understand why God allowed you to be made redundant from your job, but you do know that he sent Helen who offered you a job at the café.

Grumpy old man God

For some young people, God might just feel very out of date. They hear that he has rules that mostly say 'thou shalt not'. They conclude that the church is way out of touch with modern ideas about marriage. They read the Bible and notice that women don't get much of a say or contrast the creation story with scientific beliefs about how the universe was created. God may feel like a grumpy old man, sitting in the corner, complaining about the youth of today without bothering to understand how the world has moved on.

If you sense that your grandchild might have this view of God, again it is a question of providing balance to their views. Not many of us will feel equipped to have a debate with an impassioned 15-year-old about creation versus evolution or the church's position on gender and sexuality. However, we can talk about our own experience of God or how all his 'rules' boil down to two: loving God and loving our neighbour as ourselves, and how we've seen that revolutionise situations and even the world. We might be able to point to examples such as the church's role in overthrowing slavery in the 19th century or how Jesus upheld and honoured women and how our own church has got involved in its local community and shown people a God who loves them and who is relevant and who changes things.

You could also help rebalance this view of God by introducing your grandchild to people and places where they can hear how Christians have wrestled with big questions about God. Your pastor or youth worker might be able to recommend books or websites, or search 'apologetics' on **parentingforfaith.org** for more suggestions.

There is more on unwinding wrong views of God in the online Parenting for Faith course or in Rachel Turner's *Parenting Children for a Life of Faith*.[22]

Next steps: Have you ever noticed that any of your grand-children have a mixed-up view of God? If so, how could you help unwind that view and gently give them a more balanced view of who he is?

It's not about being an expert

Few of us are theologians or Bible scholars and it can feel hard to understand everything about God. The apostle Paul described it like this:

> Now all we can see of God is like a cloudy picture in a mirror. Later we will see him face to face. We don't know everything, but then we will, just as God completely understands us.
> 1 CORINTHIANS 13:12 (CEV)

It's important to remember, though, that we're all on a jour-ney of getting to know God better and better. It's the same process we all go on when someone new joins the family: a fiancé, perhaps, or a step-parent. At first you know little about them, but you quickly build up more information that fills in the gaps: they drive carefully; they sometimes tell risqué jokes; they were so kind when Alfie broke his leg; they are a splendid cook. You will never know everything about them, but in time, you'll have a solid bank of facts and experiences about that person which you can rely on.

Your job isn't to be an expert in who God is. Your job is to simply share what you know about God as you journey alongside your grandchildren and add to their bank of information about him. Your stories and experiences of God are so powerful for your grandchildren to hear, and each one drops another splash of truth on to their canvas.

8

Seeing God in the Bible

Family stories are important. I can still remember the stories my grandparents told me: how Sooty the cat got stuck in the coal bunker, and of how Grandma's eighth birthday present was enough wool to knit herself a new school jumper. Some of my memories impact how I behave even today. When she was a young woman, my grandma was hit on the head by a cricket ball as she walked by the ground, resulting in her losing an eye. If I'm ever near a cricket match, I remember the danger and watch out for flying balls! My grandad used to tell a tale of his first day as an office boy at the firm he stayed with for the rest of his life. His new boss deliberately left a five-shilling note for young Tommy to find when he swept the floor. Grandad's honesty in giving his boss the note back ensured that he kept his new job: a story that always springs to mind if I'm tempted to be dishonest.

Stories entertain, teach and give us a sense of who we are, and people have known this since time immemorial. Some 3,000 years ago, the psalmist Asaph wrote:

My people, hear my teaching;
  listen to the words of my mouth.
I will open my mouth with a parable;
  I will utter hidden things, things from of old –
things we have heard and known,
  things our ancestors have told us.
We will not hide them from their descendants;
  we will tell the next generation
the praiseworthy deeds of the Lord,
  his power, and the wonders he has done.
He decreed statutes for Jacob
  and established the law in Israel,
which he commanded our ancestors
  to teach their children,
so the next generation would know them,
  even the children yet to be born,
  and they in turn would tell their children.
Then they would put their trust in God
  and would not forget his deeds
  but would keep his commands.

PSALM 78:1–7

In this powerful call to action, Asaph is urging parents and grandparents to share the great stories of the Bible with the next generation and 'even the children yet to be born'. Why? So 'they would put their trust in God'.

She made a tape of stories about how God had used scripture to lead her in every decision. It is full of gems, but is testament to her dependence on God and his word and her desire to hand on the stories – to 'tell the next generation the praise-worthy deeds of the Lord'.

If you read more of Psalm 78, you'll see what Asaph wants the next generations to understand. He describes the up-and-down relationship of the Israelites with God, how they turned to him one moment and rebelled the next, yet how despite this, God kept extending his great mercy until the glorious day when he chose David to rule over the nation. He's saying: 'God kept faith with us, even when we were rebellious and ungrateful; he saved us time and time again; he forgave us and has good things for us. That's your evidence: put your trust in him!'

We have the same message, but 3,000 years later we have more to share than Asaph.

Asaph only knew of part of the story, but we have the whole story of God and us, revealed from Genesis to Revelation. It's a great overarching story of our God who creates, loves and lives with people through thick and thin, searching them out and rejoicing when they turn to him because he has a purposeful and incredible future for them, now and for eternity.[23]

For Christians, the Bible is a story that reveals the character and actions of the God who loves us and is patient with us and longs to be reconciled with us. Like Asaph, we want others to understand just how good God is. What I see in the Bible is a dramatic and compelling picture of God that draws me back to him, helps me make sense of life and gives me hope. It is central to my faith, and I want to share this with the next generations so that they too can understand who God is and put their trust in him.

The problem

I have spent a large proportion of my working life sharing the Bible with children and adults, and I've discovered it's not as easy as I once thought! For a start, it's a huge book, some parts are hard to understand, and some are decidedly inappropriate for young children. People have all sorts of assumptions about the Bible, and many don't realise it's actually one big story, instead seeing it as a series of loosely related tales. Others respect it as a source of moral truth but don't regard it as God's word.

Your grandchildren will have differing experiences of the Bible. Some will know it well; others will be barely, if at all, familiar with it. Some will have studied it at school, and heard it reduced to a series of proof texts or bite-sized passages. School assemblies, children's Bible storybooks or even Sunday School curriculums can exacerbate that, focusing on little chunks and individual stories. Some children may only know the 'big' stories: Noah, Easter, creation, Daniel, David and Christmas, and so miss the big picture of God that the Bible contains.

So how can we share the Bible well, so that people see not just the wonderful, revolutionary tale of God and us, but the little stories of who God is in joy, in misery, in hard times, in confusion, in celebrations, in the everyday and in the extraordinary – the stories that give us hope and clarity, and help us hold fast to the God we trust?

You may feel that you need a degree in theology to help your grandchildren understand the Bible. You really don't. You just need to help them see what you see.

> *Grandma wrote letters to me, telling me about what she had read in the Bible.*

In this chapter we're going to look at three ways to share the Bible with grandchildren:

- choose Bibles and Bible storybooks well
- share Bible stories well
- help them see that the God in the Bible is still the same today.

Choose Bibles and Bible story books well

There are a lot of Bibles and Bible storybooks out there! If you are fortunate enough to have a Christian bookshop near you, you'll probably find a whole selection to choose from. You could ask families at your church which Bibles they enjoy, search Christian booksellers online, or look at reviews of Bibles and other family resources on blogs, such as **thehopefilledfamily.com**. As you do so, here are some ideas to help you choose the right Bible for your grandchild.

1 **Does it work for me and my grandchild?** Are you comfortable with the content and theology? Do the pictures help you understand the stories better or distract you? There are Bibles for all sorts of children and young people: board book Bibles, cartoon Bibles,

manga and Minecraft Bibles, journalling Bibles and complete Bibles designed for children and young people with biographies, infographics and suggestions for ways to explore ideas further. Some children and young people might prefer an audio Bible.

2 **Look for Bible storybooks that tell the whole story of the Bible.** Very often stories are presented as isolated tales, rather than as part of the big story of God – the story of God who loves us, loses us, gets us back and plans a wonderful future for us. Christmas storybooks often start with Gabriel and Mary and end with a smiley baby in a manger, but miss out the reason for Jesus coming to earth in the first place or what happens next. Books like *The Jesus Storybook Bible* or *The Garden, the Curtain and the Cross* do a good job of showing how behind each individual story there is one coherent story of God and us.

3 **Discover the wonderful selection of resources available online.** There are many video versions of Bible stories on YouTube or other sites (but do check them out first to be sure you feel they are helpful). There are also a growing number of apps aimed at children, young people and families, such as Lectio for Families and Bible App for Kids, and Scripture Union have a free digital game for 8–11s called *Guardians of Ancora*, which helps children explore the Bible.

4 **Buy them a complete Bible when they are old enough – whether they want one or not.** Saying 'I want to make sure you have a Bible in case you ever need one because it's been such an important book for me. I can choose it for you, but I'd really like to know which one you'd prefer' is a powerful message for children and young people to hear.

Next steps: Think about your grandchildren. What do they think about the Bible? How could you find out? How could they access one if they don't already? What might your next steps be?

Share Bible stories well

If you are able to read Bible stories with your grandchildren, here are some tried-and-tested ideas to help them really enjoy the Bible and start to think more deeply about it. Only some of these might be relevant for your grandchildren, so feel free to pick and choose or ignore completely!

1 **Share your enthusiasm!** Show them your Bible; share why this story is your favourite or how it helps you know God better. Don't feel you have to stick to a written version of the story: use a video version if you prefer, or your grandchild might like to act it out, draw it or make an

I can remember my grandmother telling me about her favourite part of the Bible and how it helped her when her husband died.

animation as you share it together. With under-fives you can weave Bible stories into their day-to-day life: tell them the story of Zacchaeus when you spot an enormous tree or of Jesus feeding 5,000 people as you share a picnic.

2 **Make it make sense.** As you read the story, don't be afraid to stop and check in with them to explain words or ideas they don't know, such as what the tabernacle was or that the Samaritans and Jews were deadly enemies. You can remind them of where individual stories fit into the big story of the Bible; for example, before reading the story of the Exodus, you could say that the people of Israel had been stuck in Egypt for 400 years since Joseph was in charge, but God hadn't forgotten them. Or that Jesus being born isn't the end of the story – even if it is the end of their particular book – but the beginning of a whole new story that's still being written today!

3 **Be wise.** Any retelling of a Bible story inevitably means adding or changing bits. If you find something you're not sure about or know isn't true, don't be afraid to mention this to your grandchild: 'Oh, in this version of the story, they've missed out the bit in the Bible where it explains why God wanted Noah to build the ark. I wonder why they did that?' or 'Mary looks really happy about the news Gabriel brought her – do you think she would have been so happy?'

4 **Don't be scared of the tricky bits.** Some parts of the Bible may feel hard to understand or may be inappropriate to share with your grandchild, and that's okay. Be wise about what's right for your grandchild, but Bible stories can help us as we engage with tough issues, such as violence and injustice. Some things to think about:

a **It's okay to edit Bible stories, as long as we do it thoughtfully.** For example, in the story of Jericho, Rahab is called a prostitute – it would be perfectly possible to say something like 'Rahab wasn't popular. A lot of people thought she didn't live a good life and didn't like her.' If you decide to miss bits of a story out (such as Daniel's enemies being thrown into the lions' den after Daniel is rescued), think about whether missing this out changes the core of the story. If it does, it may be better not to use that story for now.

b **It's okay to say I don't know.** There will always be things in the Bible that I don't understand or which are new to me. It's helpful for children and young people to see that sometimes we all need help with the Bible. Whether you ask a friend for their opinion, turn to a podcast or check it out online, you are creating a window into what you do when you're not sure that will give your grandchild ideas for how they might grapple with bits of the Bible they don't understand.

Next steps: If you share Bible stories with your grandchildren, could any of the ideas above help you share them more fully? Are there any parts of the Bible you'd like to share with them next?

Help them see that the God in the Bible is still the same today

One of the most important things about the Bible is how it helps us see that God really gets stuck into individual people's lives. He sees Hannah's tears and answers her prayers. He provides a big fish to rescue Jonah when he ran away. He tells Paul which country to visit next.

When I see this, it teaches me about God. I realise that if I'm feeling desperate and my prayers aren't being answered, the God who answered Hannah's prayer may still answer mine. I realise that even if I've run from God like Jonah, God won't abandon me. I realise that if I need direction like Paul, God can help me.

When I understand who God *has* been in the Bible, I can see who he *is* today. That's important for grandchildren to know too, because if they grasp who God was then, they can understand that he can be that God

Grandma always made me aware of Jesus' love and that he was with me wherever I was. It was a great comfort as my family moved about often because of Dad's job. It didn't matter where we were, Jesus was still with us.

for them too. We can link the God they read about to the God who longs to know and love them today.

In a lot of the Bible, it's clear what God's doing. He talks to Noah, gives Peter a dream and writes the law down on the tablets for Moses. But there are other times when God's role in people's stories isn't always obvious. Take the story of baby Moses, for example:

> Pharaoh gave this order to all his people: 'Every Hebrew boy that is born you must throw into the Nile, but let every girl live.' Now a man of the tribe of Levi married a Levite woman, and she became pregnant and gave birth to a son. When she saw that he was a fine child, she hid him for three months. But when she could hide him no longer, she got a papyrus basket for him and coated it with tar and pitch. Then she placed the child in it and put it among the reeds along the bank of the Nile. His sister stood at a distance to see what would happen to him.
>
> Then Pharaoh's daughter went down to the Nile to bathe, and her attendants were walking along the riverbank. She saw the basket among the reeds and sent her female slave to get it. She opened it and saw the baby. He was crying, and she felt sorry for him. 'This is one of the Hebrew babies,' she said.
>
> Then his sister asked Pharaoh's daughter, 'Shall I go and get one of the Hebrew women to nurse the baby for you?'
>
> 'Yes, go,' she answered. So the girl went and got the baby's mother. Pharaoh's daughter said to her, 'Take

this baby and nurse him for me, and I will pay you.' So the woman took the baby and nursed him. When the child grew older, she took him to Pharaoh's daughter and he became her son. She named him Moses, saying, 'I drew him out of the water.'

EXODUS 1:22—2:10

Extraordinarily, even though this story is such an important part of the Bible, there is no mention of God at all! Your grandchild might read it much like a fairy story: an evil king wants to kill all the baby boys, so brave mum and big sister hide baby Moses in a basket on the river. A princess rescues him, gives him back to his mum and everyone lives happily ever after.

I'm sure that as you read the story, like me you have a running commentary in your head. 'God was protecting Moses... God must have told his mum where to put the basket in the river... God gave Miriam courage... God guided the princess down to the river that day.' We have accumulated knowledge of God that helps us fill in the gaps and shows us God's character.

One conversation that sticks in my mind is when my grandma was reading Job. She had noticed for the first time that it says that only God can walk on water and we know Jesus did, so he must be God. It made the Bible relevant and real to me.

If you are reading the story with your grandchild, you can help them fill in the gaps too. The first thing is to sometimes stop as you are reading the story and ask questions that help your grandchild think about what God was doing, feeling or thinking. So after reading Exodus 2:3, you might stop and say, 'Oh my goodness, I wonder what God felt when he saw little Moses floating in his basket.' Your grandchild might answer that God must have felt scared because Moses was so little, or that God would have been okay because he knew what would happen, or that he was pleased because Moses' mum had been obedient. Or a few verses later, you could ask: 'What was God doing as the princess was walking towards the river?' or 'I wonder what made Miriam so brave? I don't think I'd have wanted to talk to the princess!'

Do you see how that helps us see God in action? We'll never know for certain what God was doing, thinking or feeling in those gaps in the stories, but the wondering opens up ideas and conversations about who God is and how he works that can change how we see him.

Once you get used to this approach, there are so many interesting conversations waiting! 'I wonder why God chose Gideon when he was so afraid'; 'I wonder what Daniel thought as he heard the stone close him into the lions' den'; 'I wonder how God felt as he watched Jesus on the cross'; 'I wonder if I've ever been like Jonah.'

For under-fives you can use a simplified version of this idea to help them link what they hear about God from the story with who God is today. For example, if you have watched the story of Zacchaeus together you might comment: 'That story makes me think God is very kind. What do you think?' As you recreate Jesus walking on water at bath time, you could ask: 'I wonder why Peter wanted to get to Jesus so much.' Be prepared for some interesting answers, and remember it's not really about being right; it's about the wondering and conversations.

Next steps: Try reading some Bible stories and adding in the questions about what God might have been doing, feeling or thinking. If you have the opportunity, why not add one or two questions next time you are sharing a Bible story with your grandchild? If your grandchild is facing a particular situation, such as a new school or illness, or has a particular question about God, is there a Bible story that would help them explore that situation with you and God?

III

Helping grandchildren connect and cheering them on

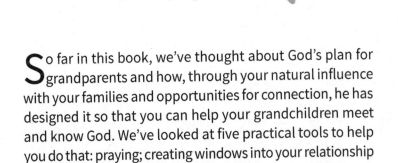

So far in this book, we've thought about God's plan for grandparents and how, through your natural influence with your families and opportunities for connection, he has designed it so that you can help your grandchildren meet and know God. We've looked at five practical tools to help you do that: praying; creating windows into your relationship with God; framing who God is; helping them get a balanced view of God; and helping them see God in the Bible.

The final part of this book is all about how you can practically support your grandchildren to meet and know God for themselves: things you can do to create opportunities for them to connect with him, how to encourage them to pray in a way that draws them close to him, how to help them engage with church – even if they don't attend – and finally, some encouragement for you as you cheer them on.

9

Moving from head to heart

In the Bible there's a beautiful picture of what a heart-to-heart connection with God is like. In Exodus 3 and 4, we read about the first time Moses meets God at the burning bush. He is puzzled, afraid, questioning and lacking confidence.[24] It seems that Moses knows who God is – he has head knowledge of God – but he doesn't seem to know him well. Later, we see a completely different person:

Now Moses used to take a tent and pitch it outside the camp some distance away, calling it the 'tent of meeting'. Anyone enquiring of the Lord would go to the tent of meeting outside the camp. And whenever Moses went out to the tent, all the people rose and stood at the entrances to their tents, watching Moses until he entered the tent. As Moses went into the tent, the pillar of cloud would come down and stay at the entrance, while the Lord spoke with Moses. Whenever the people saw the pillar of cloud standing at the entrance to the tent, they all stood and worshipped, each at the

entrance to their tent. The Lord would speak to Moses
face to face, as one speaks to a friend.
EXODUS 33:7–11

What a difference! Now Moses knew God as a friend. He had
a heart-to-heart connection with God, a profoundly deep
and sustaining relationship that served him well throughout
the turbulent years to come.

The Bible starts with a beautiful picture of God and his
newly created humans, walking and talking together in the
garden of Eden. God and his children spent time together,
enjoying each other's company. Tragically, that intimacy
was fractured when sin crept into the garden and everything changed.

God wasn't happy with this. He longed for their relationship
to be healed and restored, and the whole of the rest of the
Bible is the story of how God pursued his children, wanting
to connect with them again. There is a pivotal moment in
this story, when Jesus died:

And when Jesus had cried out again in a loud voice, he
gave up his spirit. At that moment the curtain of the
temple was torn in two from top to bottom.
MATTHEW 27:50–51

Jesus' dying changed everything. Before then, ordinary
people had no access to God at all and had to rely on a
mediator, the high priest. Only a few – prophets, priests
and kings – were granted direct access to God.[25] The high

priest literally stood between God and the people, and was the only one allowed to go behind a heavy curtain into the innermost room of the temple, directly into God's presence. Everyone else relied on the high priest to let them know what God said and to speak to God for them.

When the curtain was torn away, it signified that Jesus' death – and subsequent resurrection – had changed forever how people could encounter God. We no longer need a mediator; Jesus has made it possible for us to encounter God personally in every part of our lives. We can now connect with him individually, in a one-to-one, heart-to-heart relationship because of the death and resurrection of Jesus. As the apostle Paul says:

> Even when we were God's enemies, he made peace with us, because his Son died for us. Yet something even greater than friendship is ours. Now that we are at peace with God, we will be saved by the life of his Son. And in addition to everything else, we are happy because God sent our Lord Jesus Christ to make peace with us.
> ROMANS 5:10–11 (CEV)

This is what Jesus' death enabled, and just a few weeks later, this desire of God to reach out to all people everywhere was confirmed at Pentecost, when the Holy Spirit exploded out of a locked room into all of Jerusalem and beyond. Now everyone could have direct access to God through his Holy Spirit: the consistent presence of God with us, loving us, helping us, connecting with us, comforting, guiding and teaching us.[26]

We're all designed for connection

In chapter 2, we thought about why being connected to other people is so important: because it's when we are connected to someone that the relationship can blossom and good things follow. It's the same with God and us. God offers us so much more than just knowing *about* him; he wants us to *know* him, as a friend, a father, a saviour, a comforter and so much more. When we know him, as we connect with him, we can access all those good things he has for us.

> *'Gana' heard God's voice everywhere. 'God told me to take that bit of salmon out of the freezer and give it to...' It wasn't so much knowing that she was a Christian, as witnessing this incredible relationship with God who directed her daily.*

Just as we have individual preferences for how we connect with others and communicate with them, the same is true of how we connect with and communicate with God. Our whole bodies seem designed to help us connect with him: our senses, our mind and even our emotions come into play. We learn, as we go along in our journeys with God, what helps us draw close to him.

I have a friend who just likes to sit and write as she connects with God. I know that I connect with him best when I walk alone with no one else to hear me tell him everything. Others find him in the stillness of a cathedral or as the ancient words of the liturgy wash over them. Some chatter to him as they drive, others feel God close as they listen to worship or receive the Eucharist. Others are invigorated by a robust discussion in home group, understanding God better as they wrestle with scripture.

The God who made each one of us loves to connect with us in ways that suit our personalities and preferences. He wants to connect with all of us, including our grandchildren. They may just need someone to show them how.

Below we're going to look at two things you can do to help your grandchildren connect with God:

- create windows into and frame how you connect with God yourself
- help them understand what prayer is.

Create windows into and frame how you connect with God

Your grandchildren will be aware of how you connect with people around you. They'll hear conversations, but also watch you hug their mum or know that you've just sent a text to your friend. They'll see that even when you're just sitting next to someone on the sofa, you can still be connecting with them. They are probably much less likely to know how you connect with God.

If you can create windows into and frame how you connect with God, you'll open a whole pile of possibilities for your grandchild. They might never have thought about the possibility of connecting with him! And even if they have, by getting glimpses of how you connect with him, you will be widening their experience and giving them ideas to try for themselves. It's not about teaching them all the possible ways God might connect with them; rather, it's helping them see your experience so they have a jumping-off point to explore what it might look like for them and God.

There are lots of ideas for doing this in chapters 5 and 6, but here are some examples of what it might look like for connecting with God.

- **Talk about connecting with God.** This may be an idea that your grandchild has never considered before. Use whatever language reflects your experience. I talk about 'connecting', but you might say something like 'feel God's presence' or 'spend time with him.' Whatever phrase you use, you will be opening their mind to the idea that God is a person who wants to hang out with us – and that's brilliant! You could drop into conversation a question: did you know that God wants to connect with us? Or, if you are in church, you could point out others connecting: 'That person looks like they are connecting with God as they sing'; or mention that you like to go to home group on Thursdays because it's a place which helps you feel close to God.

- **Let them see or understand how and why you connect.** Simply add in the 'God bit' that's in your head. You could explain that you felt so frazzled you needed to go for a walk to spend time with God. As you listen to a favourite hymn, you might whisper: 'I love this hymn – it always reminds me that God draws me close to him whenever I need him.' Allow them to see you listening to your daily Bible reading or taking a few moments to be with God.

- **Share stories of how you connect.** These might be stories of times you connected with God and the difference it made: when you felt unhappy and he comforted you, or how he highlighted this verse from scripture that changed a decision, or that when you share Communion at church, you always draw close to God and feel his presence.

- **If you can, create opportunities for them to connect alongside you.** If you journal and your grandchild is interested, you might buy them a notebook and invite them to read scripture and journal alongside you. You might invite a grandchild to come along to a service that particularly helps you connect to God. You could send a grandchild a copy of a book you're reading that helps you feel closer to God, or send them a link to a worship song that draws you into God's presence.

Next steps: Think about your grandchildren. Do you think they know the difference between knowing *about* God and *knowing* God as a friend? Which of the ideas above might you try?

Help grandchildren understand what prayer is

Prayer probably plays a large part in your life. It's something many of us depend on as we live our daily lives. We've learned that prayer is so many things: a practical place to find guidance and support; a way to express our innermost feelings to God; a comfort; and so much more. I turn to prayer almost without thinking, knowing that my heavenly Father is there. Sometimes I rely on the Lord's Prayer, or spend time bringing people and situations before God; sometimes I just chat to him as I go about my ordinary day, or fire up 'arrow prayers'[27] in response to a situation.

Children and teens are exposed to the idea of prayer from their earliest years, whether that's the hands-together-eyes-closed prayer of school assemblies, the 'thoughts and prayers' that are commonly expressed by public figures in response to a national tragedy, or bedtime prayers at home. But what they might not realise is that prayer, at its heart, is a way God has given us to connect with him. Prayer is the offer of heart-to-heart conversation with a God who loves us, cares for us and who has promised to take part in the conversation too.

Here are three ideas for helping grandchildren see and understand what prayer can be like:

- unwind any wrong ideas they might have about prayer
- create windows into and frame your own experience of prayer
- create opportunities for them to pray.

Unwind any wrong ideas about prayer

 In chapter 7 we thought about how children having a mixed-up view of God can stop them wanting to relate to him. This can also affect if and how they pray. For example, if they believe God is angry with them or far away, they may be reluctant to try talking to God or they may want an adult to intercede for them. You can unwind that by sharing your experiences, or reminding them that God wants them to pray about everything because he cares about them.[28]

Children may also have had all sorts of experiences and information about prayer that shapes how they feel about it. Some may be helpful, and some not. Some children and young people may not know much about prayer at all. They may have been

> I remember them affirming me when I had a picture age seven and told them I'd just made it up. They said: 'Jesus lives inside of you so you won't be making it up as he is there speaking to you.'

told that there are special times and ways to pray – you need to sit still, or it's something done at bedtime. Many people's experience of prayer is that it's led from the front and is a one-way flow of information. Some may not know that you can pray about anything and that even small or inconsequential matters are important to God.

These views can prevent them from accessing the full beauty and power of prayer. If you spot any of these, the easiest way to rebalance them is to share your own experiences of prayer. Telling a grandchild that you talk to God in the loo will certainly challenge any belief that there are proper places to pray!

Next steps: Think about your grandchildren. What do they think about prayer? How could you find out? Do you think they may have any wrong ideas about prayer? How could you rebalance these?

Create windows into and frame how and why you pray

I have a friend, Hayley, who became a Christian late in life, having had no experience of God at all. We both joined a WhatsApp group to pray for someone who was undergoing complicated surgery. We received prayer updates daily, many of which were really detailed, asking for specific outcomes, while others dealt with the practicalities, that the cab would arrive on time, that God would sort out someone to look after the cat – all those little details we know God cares about. Some people wrote their prayers and hallelujahs and emojis in the chat. A few weeks later, Hayley and I talked about the WhatsApp group. 'I had no idea that you could pray like that!' she said. Because she had seen glimpses of how others prayed, Hayley now had a totally different idea of how she could pray.

It's eye-opening for people who might not know much about prayer to hear the authentic prayers of ordinary people, and one of the simplest ways to help your grandchildren see what prayer means to you is for you to create windows into how you pray.

Your grandchildren probably know that you pray, but they may not know what you pray about or how you do it. They might not even know what praying sounds like or that it can be a free and easy conversation with God where he tells you things back. By deliberately creating windows into your prayer life with God, you can change that. As you pray aloud, your grandchild will know what prayer sounds like and can have a go themselves. If you mention that some-times when you pray it's like words hitting the ceil-ing but at other times you just know God's heard you because you get a reply straight back, your grand-child will know not to be discouraged if they don't hear God straightaway. Allowing your grandchild to spot the prayer list on the fridge or hear your daily prayer app helps them understand that prayer is important to you and there are different ways to do it.

> *I remember my gran, who was a nervous driver, always pulling into the supermarket and praying out loud that God would help her find a wee easy spot to park in. She hated parking. And every time she found the spot she would give thanks to God. I remember learning that God is in the ordinary too.*

You can also frame how prayer works for you. Sharing stories of when you've prayed and what happened will probably be fascinating for your grandchild. Learning that you asked

God's opinion before proposing to your spouse or that you changed job because you believe you heard God telling you to, might paint a completely different picture of prayer for your grandchild, as well as inspiring them to ask him things too. Open up conversations about prayer, and share how different people prayed in the Bible: Jesus retreated into the hills to spend time with God; Hezekiah shared a scary letter with God; Hannah wept in the tabernacle; Nehemiah sent a quick arrow prayer when he didn't know how to answer the king; Deborah prayed as she danced and sang; God had whole conversations with Abraham and even wrestled with Jacob.[29]

Of course, there can be a big jump between knowing that God speaks and being able to recognise his voice when he speaks to us. If your grandchild is new to the idea of God speaking to people, they may find it difficult to think what it would be like, unable to imagine the creativity of God. You can share how you recognise God's voice when you pray so you can help your grandchildren understand that God does speak to us. Even if your grandchild is around people who believe and experience God speaking today, they may still not be clear about what it's actually like or how to recognise it, because Christians often use vague language to describe how God communicates with them, such as 'I had a sense that...' or 'The Lord led me...'

They talked about how prayer had helped them through things so I knew that if I was ever in difficulty my first response should be to pray.

As you create windows into how you recognise God's voice, you might be giving your grandchild a whole new set of ideas. For example, if you heard God speak through a passage from the Bible, that is helpful for them to hear. If you had a gut feeling that God wanted you to go round to Mrs White's house or had a picture in your mind that helped you understand him, when you share what happened and how you knew it was God, you are opening their eyes to new possibilities. However you hear God's voice or know his will, however you know what he is saying to you or know how he has responded to your prayer, create windows into and frame that for them.

Next steps: Have you created any windows into prayer for your grandchildren? Is there anything you'd like them to know? How could you create a window into that? What stories or pictures of prayer might be helpful for them?

Create opportunities for grandchildren to pray

If it is appropriate in your family, you can look for ways to create opportunities for your grandchildren to pray. You'll come up with your own ideas, but here are some to get you started.

- **Ask them to pray for you.** About the big and the little. If they are willing, you might text them prayer requests or update them when you chat.

- **Suggest they pray about things on their mind.** In their conversations with you, they may mention a situation that angers them, a friendship problem or something they are worried about. You can simply suggest that, as well as talking to you about it, they might want to tell God they are anxious about going to Dad's place at the weekend or angry about the news item they've just read. Encourage them as they pray to leave space for God to speak back.

- **Pray at bedtimes and mealtimes.** For some families these are natural times to pray. If you are used to set prayers, you might want to consider praying in a more informal way; you can also invite your grandchildren to be the ones who pray.

> I vividly recall one time staying over at my grandparents and they invited me to join them for their evening prayer time. I found that a really helpful insight into how to have an active faith life as a married couple.

- **Take them to places where people pray.** Whether it's the quiet of a cathedral, a prayer meeting or a pilgrimage, seeing how others pray will give your grandchildren new ideas and opportunities to join in.

- **Point them to resources that may help them pray.** As well as prayer apps designed for families and children and teens, there are books on prayer for all ages. Browse a Christian bookshop or ask for ideas from others to see if anything catches your eye.

- **Feed back to them.** If your grandchildren are praying for you, update them on the situation – what God did and how you believe prayer made a difference. There's nothing more encouraging to a beginning pray-er! If they have told you they are praying for something, from time to time you might want to ask how that went.

Next steps: Are any of these ideas for creating opportunities for grandchildren to discover more about prayer appropriate for your family? What might you like to try?

Finally

At Parenting for Faith, we have some suggestions for how, if you are able, to actively coach your grandchildren in prayer. You can encourage them to develop their own conversational prayer life with God. You can see what that might look like in the appendix, 'Getting started with chat and catch'.

Not all grandparents are in a position to talk about prayer directly with grandchildren or have enough time with them to talk at length about praying. If that is the case for you, be confident that, by creating windows into the way you catch from God and sharing stories of times you caught God's voice, you will be giving your grandchildren – maybe for the first time – a picture of a God who not only speaks but wants to speaks to us. You will also be giving them ideas for how they can pray themselves and building an expectation that God will talk back, all the time adding those little splashes to their canvas.

Opening up the Tardis

When *Doctor Who* first aired in 1963, blue police boxes were a common sight on Britain's streets. These were like miniature police stations for bobbies on the beat, containing a telephone connected to the local police station, a stool, a small desk and very little else. So when, in the first episode, innocent bystanders wandered into the Tardis, a time-travelling machine disguised as an ordinary police box, they were shocked to learn it was not what it seemed: extraordinarily larger on the inside than on the outside and containing a feast of wonders. Over the years, viewers have discovered that the Tardis houses a seemingly endless collection of rooms: not just those they might have expected like the console room, bedrooms and libraries, but also swimming pools, gardens, an observatory and an art gallery, and even a laundromat, a croquet court and a sun room.

I wonder if church is a bit of a Tardis for many people – a building they recognise and think they understand, but with no idea of the wonders it contains. Far from just conducting weddings, funerals and Sunday services, our churches are so much more on the inside than you would think from the outside: food banks, toddler groups, pastoral

care, parenting courses, worship, debt advice, young people's groups, campaigns for social justice, Fairtrade champions, communities where everyone is welcome – a veritable
feast of wonders.

For those of us who love and worship God, it is also a place
where the kingdom of God is realised, home for those who
choose to make it so and a powerful force for good in its
local community and the world at large. It's where we can
learn more about God and draw near to him; it's where we
are loved and encouraged; and it's where we are equipped
to take part in God's plan for our communities and the world.

Although going to church isn't a prerequisite for being a
Christian, it is something which is valuable for Christians
to do. God brought the very first Christians together into a
church not just so they could better meet and know him
there, but because church
provides us with a family to
encourage, love and chal-
lenge us in our Christian
journey. Wherever I have
travelled, I have found a
church, a home away from
home, where I am instantly
loved and known – simply
because we share a love of
Christ.

*Their services were very
'other' – Gaelic-speaking
Catholic mass – but the
fact they went at all,
I think, made church feel
like a normal thing to me.
So when I decided to start
going to church I at least
knew what to expect.*

No wonder, then, that we want those we love to understand
how amazing church is. What I long for my daughter is that

she knows that being part of a church is integral to her well-being; a place of companionship, challenge, comfort and purpose, a place where she can not only meet God but also be part of his great call for us to join him in transforming the world. My prayer, as I write this, is that all your grandchildren will discover this beauty and power of church.

The first visitors to the Tardis thought they knew what it was – but there was so much more for them to learn. Whether or not your grandchildren go to church, you can help them see what you love and value about church and help them make the shift from church being 'somewhere my grandparents go' to seeing it as interesting, powerful and a possibility for them too.

Here are two ways to help your grandchildren see the beauty and power of church:

- create windows into and frame the power of church for you
- make visits to church count.

Create windows into and frame the power of church for you

I wonder why church is important to you. For me, I love the community I find there and the opportunities it provides to worship God in ways different from how I worship alone. Others at my church are fierce champions of the poor and persecuted; some find it a place where they can dig deep into scripture; some find respite from their day-to-day struggles; some serve weekly and daily, finding their purpose in the kingdom of God there.

If we can create windows into and frame why church is important to us, we can help people get a real insight into the power and beauty of church that can be transformative. All of us who have watched *Doctor Who* know now that the Tardis is far more important than it appears on the outside: it is a place of refuge in a crisis, it contains answers (and questions) and it has so much that The Doctor and his companions need. It is very far removed from the boring blue police box it appears to be from the outside.

Whatever your grandchildren's situation now, you can help to build a foundation of truth about church that they can draw on later in life – when they are considering whether to go to church after they leave home; when, as new parents, they join a church toddler group; in times of crisis; or simply because they have questions that need answering. What you show them and how you talk about church will shape their view of church and open their eyes to new possibilities for them.

> *My grandparents used to go to this very rural small church in South Africa, and I was always fascinated about how much they loved the church they went to and the community they had there.*

How can you do this? It's just more of creating windows and framing – which we explored in chapters 5 and 6. All you are doing is trying to reveal more of what church is for you.

This might be simply adding in who God is and what he's doing into your ordinary conversations – just adding the 'God bit'.

- At church on a Sunday morning, you might have heard something in the sermon that really helped you. You could create a window into that by saying: 'At church on Sunday, the sermon was so interesting – there was one phrase the preacher used that felt like God had written it just for me and I was so grateful.'

- When you're talking about your recent holiday, you might add: 'We went to the church near the caravan park – and it was so lovely – a real home from home. I love that about church – wherever you go, you have a family that welcomes you.'

- If your church is making a difference in the local community – whether hosting a knife amnesty, replanting wildlife verges or holding a fun day for local children – you can create a window for a grandchild that reveals how God wants the church to be active and transformative. 'I'm so pleased that we are helping to organise the knife amnesty at church – it's a really practical way to show God's love for this town.'

Your grandchildren are probably aware that you do church activities, but they may not know what motivates you to do them. When you are talking about church, you can also explain the 'whys' as well as the 'whats', so that they understand that church isn't just another club or something to keep you busy: it's something that has real impact on you and helps you understand and connect with God.

- For example, say you help out at the toddler group on a Monday. Your granddaughter may know that you help out, but you can also give her the 'why': 'I went to help out at toddlers this morning. It's utterly exhausting chasing the little ones, but I get such a buzz out of knowing that the mums who come get some of God's love there.'

- Imagine a grandchild wants to pop in on Monday or Tuesday next week. You might just say, 'Tuesday would be better', but by adding the why – 'because it's my Bible study group on Monday and I love chewing over what the Bible means with my friends' – you give a glimpse of how church helps you wrestle with scripture.

- Even if you're not entirely enthusiastic about church, you can still communicate how significant church is for you. Imagine it's the rugby world cup and a big game clashes with church: 'I'd

My grandmother spoke of attending Sunday school every week as she grew up and she spoke of happy memories of that. It intrigued me as I'd never experienced it.

really rather be watching the rugby this morning, but I know that if I don't go to church I'll miss worshipping God' is a thought-provoking comment for someone who knows how much you love rugby!

Encourage questions and conversations about church too, and as you give your grandchildren little insights into what you value and love about church, you are opening their eyes to the possibility that church could be a good place for them too.

Next steps: Why is church important to you? What would you like your grandchildren to understand about church? How could you create windows into or frame that for them?

Make visits to church count

If you are able to take your grandchildren to church – whether that's a regular Sunday service or something like Messy Church – there are some simple things you can do to make sure your grandchildren have a good experience of church and spot why church is so significant for you and how God is present and active there.

Do your prep

You're probably really used to preparing for a day out with children – and depending on the age of your grandchildren, a visit to church may not be so different! Here are some things to think about.

- **Get the information you need.** If there are children's groups or a crèche, what ages do they cover? When do they go out? Where can I change the baby or get a glass of water? If it's a eucharistic service, where Communion is taken, what do children do? If it's Messy Church, do I need to stay with my grandchild all the time or can they go around the tables on their own?

- **Take what you need.** It's always worth packing a small bag with what you need and what you think you might not, such as snacks, drinks, a child's Bible, pens and paper and quiet toys.

> *She was always there. She made it fun and we could snuggle up with her and eat the sweets she brought us during the sermon when there was no Sunday school.*

- **Decide on your boundaries.** Do you want them to go to the children's groups or can they stay with you if they want to? During worship, do you expect them to stand and sing with you or can they sit down or move around? During the sermon, are you happy with them reading quietly or playing a quiet game? Be aware of what you are comfortable with and what would make you feel stressed.

- **Prepare your grandchild.** Depending on the age and nature of your grandchild, and if they are unused to church, you may need to do no more than say, 'We're going to Messy Church on Tuesday'. Some children may have questions they need to ask or feel more comfortable if they've seen the outside or even inside of the building first. Fill them in on what will happen, how long it will take and what they will be doing.

Frame the service for them

 There are all sorts of things that happen in church services which might not make sense to someone who is new to church. We have special words we use, like 'Eucharist'; we read some bits from a screen or from books; people stand up and sit down at particular times; we sing to an invisible person; we may even put money on a plate and have a long list of notices.

Think of yourself as a safari guide. During a safari, the guide has two functions. They have to share practical information to help guests navigate the journey well, and they have to point out the wonderful animals and birds that the guests might otherwise not see. So during the service, you can do both of those things. You can frame what's happening now and what's happening next for your grandchild so that the service makes sense, and you can point out where God is busy and active.

To help your grandchild navigate the service well, you can add simple explanations to help them make sense of what's going on; for example: 'Everyone is standing up now so they can get ready to sing'; 'People are bowing their heads so they can listen carefully to the prayers'; or 'The priest is making the shape of the cross with his hand as he asks God to bless everyone before we leave.'

Then you can frame, or point out, where you see God busy and active. Don't feel the pressure to frame every bit; share what you know and see. For example:

- 'When I do these actions with my body it's like a language, telling God how much I love him.'
- 'Communion is a special tiny meal God invented to help us remember that Jesus died on the cross so we could be friends with God again.'
- 'I know these notices are very long, but I love hearing how many different things people at church are doing to share God's love.'
- 'Sometimes I don't understand everything in the talk, but I always listen carefully to try to spot anything God particularly wants me to hear.'

Do what you do with God in front of your grandchildren – as far as you can!

We know that one of the most powerful ways people learn is by watching and copying other people. So as far as possible, do what you normally do with God in a church service when your grandchildren are there. If you're jiggling a fractious

My grandma always knelt to pray in church. I remember being quite young and not understanding why, but when she did it, she looked so focused on prayer and it seemed such an intimate moment between her and God.

baby or drawing a picture with a bored eight-year-old, you won't have the luxury of uninterrupted God-and-me time, but where you can, let them see your normal rhythms and patterns of connecting with God.

This may mean quickly explaining: 'I'll draw a bit more in a minute, but right now, can we just sit quietly while I listen to the notices so I know what our church family are doing?' or 'I always like to write down anything important I hear the preacher say – would you like a piece of paper and a pen to do the same?' If you serve, let them help you if you can: stand alongside you to help welcome people; come up to stand with you as you read or lead intercessions; carry a plate of biscuits as you pass round cups of tea and coffee.

Debrief with them afterwards

Debriefing is simply a way to open up conversations about church so that your grandchildren have a chance to process what they experienced and ask any questions they have.

Start by sharing a little bit about your own experience of church that day: what helped you connect with God, how you felt, anything that made you think or people you really appreciated. Comments such as 'That sermon – kapow! – it really helped me realise that God can mend broken hearts' or 'It was lovely seeing Glenda

After church I used to go with my grandad to check on his shop. He would always slip me a chocolate bar and we would talk about what I had learned in Sunday school.

again, she always has some wise words for me' create a window for grandchildren into the power and significance of church for you, as well as what God was doing.

Then ask some open questions to invite your grandchild into a conversation – and be prepared to answer them yourself! For example:

- Is there anything buzzing in your brain from church today?
- Did you spot God doing anything?
- What bits of today did you enjoy? Or not enjoy?
- Do you have any questions about church today?

Next steps: Which of these ideas might you want to try if you take your grandchildren to church?

For many of us, church is central to our lives as Christians and we long for others to know and love church as we do. If your grandchildren don't attend church, that can be a source of sadness, but please remember how influential you are! By giving your grandchildren glimpses of the importance of church for you, by helping them understand its impact on you, your community and the world, you are showing them that church is relevant, powerful and transformative – the sort of community they might one day want to belong to. You are giving them information and choices they might not otherwise have.

11

In it for the long haul

Whenever I get a new car, one of the first things I do is to look at the handbook. I'm not a very techy person and certainly don't understand the combustion engine – or any modern variation of it! So I look at the handbook to make sure I know the basics: how to make the lights work, what fuel it needs, how to move the seats forward and back – all the bits required to help me jump into the car and get going. To be honest, I skim read most of it, because lots of it just isn't relevant at that moment.

From time to time, though, I revisit the handbook, to see if there's anything in it that I need to know now. What is the recommended ratio of water to screenwash now that it's winter? The car is choc-a-bloc with heavy cases for a long journey – do I need to change the tyre pressure? Or my car nightmare: what's that flashing symbol that's just lit up as I drive down the motorway?

Treat this book like a handbook for Christian grandparenting. You won't need all of it straightaway, but it's worth reading through to get the basics. Then, as things change, come back to it. Your grandchildren will grow and change. You'll change. There'll be different times and seasons. This book is for you to use as you need, and it's yours for the long haul.

You may be interested in some of the other Parenting for Faith resources as you grandparent your grandchildren. If they are little, we have a book that explores how to help 0–3s meet and know God: *Babies and Toddlers: Nurturing your child's spiritual life* by Rachel Turner. If you have teen or young adult grandchildren, *Parenting Teens for a Life of Faith* will help you apply the tools we've talked about in this book to your older grandchildren. For a deeper dive into the principles of parenting and grandparenting children for faith, there's *Parenting Children for a Life of Faith*, an omnibus edition that includes two extra books on how to help children develop a godly core of confidence, and how to help them find their purpose in God. Finally, the website **parentingforfaith.org** has many articles as well as access to video courses on parenting for faith.

Our prayer is that this book has encouraged you with the fact that you can help your grandchildren meet and know God. Remember, God's design for grandparenting for faith, just like his design for parenting for faith, is not intended to be difficult or overwhelming. As you pray for your grandchildren, check in with God on your next steps. Then grab your toolkit of grandparenting for faith skills and be encouraged!

Don't journey alone

Life always seems easier when we do it with other people. I remember the relief when, on taking my newborn to her first baby group, I discovered that she wasn't the only baby to scream inconsolably and then got some new ideas to try from the other mums. You might already be chatting to other Christian grandparents, but if not, why not invite one or two round for coffee or even start a grandparenting movement in your church? Share your stories, pray for your grandchildren and encourage and support each other as you grandparent for faith through the ups and downs, tears and triumphs, and ordinary, everyday life.

We'll end where we began

Remember the poppies. Discipling your grandchildren is simply about journeying alongside them and helping them gradually paint a picture of who God is and who he wants them to be, and encouraging them to meet and know him for themselves. Every time you share a story about who God is, point out what God is doing or let your grandchildren see you connecting with God yourself, you're dropping another splash of colour on to their canvas. You might not be able to paint the whole picture for them, but your splashes of colour will join splashes that others and God himself are adding.

I'll leave the last word to Katherine Bergin, marriage and family life advisor for the diocese of Arundel and Brighton:

You're laying groundwork that you may never see the results for by being yourself, by being a faith-filled person and living your life according to the way you think you should... It's not rocket science. It's being yourself, loving God and sharing that in the best ways you can.[30]

Getting grandchildren started with 'chat and catch'

In chapter 8 we thought about prayer: how it is a two-way conversation with God; how we articulate our prayers in many different ways; how we can 'hear' God's voice in different ways; how it brings hope, guidance, comfort and so much more.

 At Parenting for Faith, we have found that by using the phrase 'chat and catch' for prayer, it helps children and young people see prayer in a whole new light. The word 'chat' encompasses everything from a lighthearted conversation with a friend to a serious discussion with a wise counsellor. The word 'catch', which we use for however the individual 'hears' God's voice, frees children and young people from the impression that we will physically hear God's voice. We can 'chat' to God, and be ready to 'catch' his reply.

If it's helpful, there are two sessions on 'chat' and 'catch' in the Parenting for Faith course, which you can watch online at **parentingforfaith.org/course**.

Introducing grandchildren to 'chat'

These are some straightforward steps you can take to coach your grandchild in how to chat to God about everything.

1 Talk about what chatting is: it's how we talk to our friends or family, about big things and little things. It can be a serious conversation, a shared joke or a quick word. Explain that we can chat to God in the same way. He loves to hear everything on our hearts.

2 Tell them that you are going to suggest some things for them to tell God in their head or write down or draw (or however they can or prefer to communicate). Then give them some suggestions; mix up big issues and little things, feelings and experiences, fears and joy so they understand that it's okay to talk to God about it all. For example, tell God:

- your favourite colour
- a pet you'd love to have one day
- one thing you have to do every day you wish you didn't have to
- the name of your favourite YouTuber
- one thing you like about yourself
- one thing that makes you really sad

- a joke
- what you love about your family
- something you'd like to change
- how you feel about him (you can say anything!)
- the name of someone who hurts your feelings
- the bravest person you know.

Tailor the questions to the age and circumstances of your grandchildren; this is simply a way of giving them permission to talk to God about everything and experience what that is like. If this is a new idea for you, have a go yourself first so that you can see what it feels like and the impact it has. Encourage them that they can chat to God about anything, anytime and anywhere, reminding them that if something is important to them, it's important to God and he wants to hear it.

3 Then simply encourage them to chat to God. As you collect an excited five-year-old from school, you might say: why don't you chat to God and tell him what you did today? At bedtime, leave your grandchildren with a reminder that God loves to hear all about their day, so why not chat to him for as long as you want to? Chat to God yourself in front of them and keep on framing how and why you chat to God.

Introducing grandchildren to 'catch'

You may know from your own experience how you hear God's voice: maybe a strong impression on your heart, or a thought that pops into your head, a dream, a verse from the Bible that stands out to you. There are so many ways God speaks to us, sometimes instigating conversation and sometimes replying to people's words.

1 Talk about how we know that God 'chats' back to us. You can create windows and frame your experiences of hearing God or point to examples in the Bible: Jesus uses the image of the good shepherd whose sheep know and hear his voice. Jeremiah says that God will tell us 'great and unsearchable things you do not know'.[31]

2 It can be helpful to explain to children that because God wants us to be friends with him, he made our bodies so that they are able to help us catch everything he wants to say to us, even when he doesn't speak in words. So there are different ways that we can catch from God:

- **Through scripture and wise people (2 Chronicles 34:19–21; Exodus 18).** We may sense that God is highlighting a particular verse of the Bible for us, or realise that God has used someone to speak his wisdom to us.

- **With our brains (Acts 10:9–12; Acts 2:17–18, 9:10; Amos 4:13).** We may see a picture or a movie in our mind of something God wants to show us. Some people 'hear' words in their heads or even have whole conversations there. Other people find ideas from God pop into their mind.

- **With our eyes and ears (Daniel 5; 1 Samuel 3).** Some people may hear God audibly or see something that others don't see.

- **With our skin (Psalm 39:2–3; 1 Kings 8:10–11).** People may feel warmth or tingling, or feel God physically close to them.

- **With our emotions (Philippians 4:7; 1 Peter 1:9).** We may feel a sense of peace or disquiet or 'holy anger' as God uses our emotions to communicate with us.

- **With our guts (Mark 11:15–18; John 4:1–9; 1 Corinthians 12:8).** People may feel a strong instinct that something is wrong, or that they need to say something.

- **In our dreams (Acts 16:6–10; Matthew 2:12).**

How you share these will depend on your circumstances and your grandchild's age and personality. With your three-year-old you might just say, 'Did you know, God sometimes puts pictures in our heads?' and reserve a fuller conversation for your twelve-year-old. You might have a curious grandchild who'd love to talk about this, or you may just tuck these ideas away, waiting for the right moment.

3 Then you can help them get started catching from God. If this is new to your grandchildren, the easiest way to introduce them to catching from God is just to get

started. Make sure that they are aware of the different ways people catch from God, and then ask a question that doesn't have a right answer. For example, 'Ask God what game he'd like to play with you' or 'What is God's favourite place?' If you feel it's right, encourage them to carry on the conversation they and God have just started: 'Gosh, that's interesting. Why not ask God why he likes Italy?'

4 Just like chat, create opportunities for your grandchild to continue discovering how they catch from God. If they are worried about something or have a question, you can suggest they check in with God and see if they catch what he says. If you're reading a book together, you might want to ask God a question about the story and see what you catch. You can ask God a question about the news article you've just watched, or ask God what his favourite thing in the park is.

On the Parenting for Faith website we have a free download with 101 suggestions for ways to get children and young people chatting and catching with God (**parentingforfaith. org/101-conversations**). This will help you carry on creating opportunities for your grandchildren to experience the wonder of prayer and learn to recognise the ways they and God communicate best.

Dealing with disappointment and discernment

Inevitably, your grandchild will have times when they won't catch from God. I imagine that, like me, you've had times when you haven't caught God's voice, and you might have felt hurt or disappointed. Some children find it hard to get started with catching or your grandchild might have asked God something and not caught anything.

If so, it can be helpful to remind them that just like babies learn to recognise different people's voices, we are all learning to recognise God's voice and sometimes get it wrong. You can remind them that God 'talks' in all sorts of ways and remind them of the main ways we've talked about. You can encourage them by explaining that sometimes you don't catch either, but you also know that he loves you, is talking to you and wants us to know his voice. Sharing stories of times you've prayed and caught nothing back helps grandchildren realise that not catching is a normal part of a Christian's experience, and not a disaster or a rejection.

If we are teaching our grandchildren to catch God's voice, we also need to help them learn to discern if they have caught his voice correctly. There are some important things we know about God which can reassure us.

- He has given us the Bible, which is like a light for us and gives us understanding (Psalm 119:105, 125), the Holy Spirit to guide us into all truth and to lead us (John 16:13), and Jesus to show us what he is like (John 14:9)

- Jesus said that the sheep recognise their shepherd's voice: God intends for us to be able to recognise his voice (John 10).

- Father God is a good father – he always loves, always is truthful and doesn't set out to confuse or upset (1 John 4:7–12; John 14:6; 1 Corinthians 14:33).

- He loves to give us wisdom (James 1:5) and has placed us in communities where we can seek wisdom (Colossians 3:16)

It can also help to remember that there are only three answers to the question 'Do you think that is from God?' – yes, no and maybe (like traffic lights). So when your grandchild comes to you and says 'I think God is saying…', there are also some really simple questions we can ask to help them work out if what they've caught is from God.

- Does it sound like something God would say – does it fit with what you know about God?
- Does it feel right? Do you feel peaceful about what you've caught?
- Would you like to check it out with someone wise?
- Do you have any more questions about it – why not go back and chat to God again?

If your grandchild isn't sure whether they have caught from God, reassure them that that is okay and that it's important for us to make sure we know it is God's voice before acting on it. Remind them that God is patient and kind and if he has something he wants us to know he will keep on telling us, and we won't miss out just because we're still learning to recognise his voice. Similarly, if they decide that what they caught wasn't from God, reassure them that they didn't do anything wrong – again, it's all part of this process of learning to recognise God's voice.

Small group notes

Thank you for reading this book!

Below we've added some suggestions for how you might explore the ideas we've talked about with others: maybe a partner or friend, or a small group. We have written these notes for grandparents, but you may also be journeying with extended family members, godparents or people whose role is to support grandparents. Please do adapt the sessions accordingly.

If you're meeting for just a short time, we suggest you use the opening question, key points from the chapter and one or more of the discussion questions before praying together. If you have longer, feel free to add any of the other elements: treat them as a pick-and-mix to find the combination that suits you best. We've added timings to give you an idea of how long each element might take. The sessions will work best if everyone has their own copy of the book and reads the relevant chapters beforehand.

This really isn't about getting things right or wrong. It's about exploring what grandparenting looks like for you in your unique situation. You will all have wisdom and experience to bring to the table. Remember that God is already at work in your grandchildren's lives and will always have a next step for you.

Enjoy listening to each other, and to God, as you pursue your grandparenting journey!

Introduction and chapter 1: God invented grandparents

Gather (5–15 min). A chance to catch up and share a cuppa.

Welcome and recap (5–10 min). Introduce yourself and your grandchildren. Share the aims of the group – for example, to support each other, share ideas, pray for each other and our grandchildren. Let people know this is a safe place to share about their families. To keep it that way, ask them to keep anything that is shared confidential.

Opening question (5–10 min). What are grandparents for?

Share the key ideas from the introduction and chapter (5 min).

- God invented grandparents – they are part of his design for how grandchildren learn to meet and know him.
- Discipleship is a gradual process over time.
- It's a process of 'adding your splashes to the canvas' (see page 11) that God, your grandchildren and others are painting.
- We can share faith like we share other passions and interests.
- Both the secular and the religious research are clear: grandparents are very influential in the lives of their grandchildren.

Individual reflection (5 min). What are your hopes and dreams for your grandchildren?

Discussion questions (10–15 min). Choose one or more of the questions to help people explore the ideas further.

- How did your grandparents influence you? (Be mindful that not everyone may have known their grandparents or have had a positive experience of them.)
- How do you feel about the idea of sharing your faith with your grandchildren?
- Did anything about the research into the influence of grandparents surprise you?
- What passions have been passed down in your family? How did that happen?

Bible study (10–15 min). How did Jesus disciple people? Choose some or all of the following passages – what can we learn from them?

- Mark 1:35–37
- Matthew 8:23–27
- Mark 10:32–34
- Luke 10:1
- Matthew 9:9
- Luke 11:1–11
- John 9:1–7

Next steps (5 minutes). Allow people time to think about one or two things they want to take away or try from this session. One idea to suggest: take a few moments before the next session to pray about each of their grandchildren and ask God to show them how they already influence them and what their next steps might be.

Pray for each other and each other's grandchildren (5–10 min).

Chapter 2: Connection is key

Gather (5–15 min). A chance to catch up and share a cuppa.

Welcome and recap (5–10 min). Welcome and introduce anyone new. Recap the previous session and ask for any feedback. How are people feeling about the idea that they are an important part of God's plan for their grandchildren meeting and knowing him? Have they done anything differently as a result?

Opening question (5–10 min). Think about a family member or friend you felt close to when you were growing up. What made you feel connected to them?

Share the key ideas from the chapter (5 min).
- Grandparents and grandchildren have a natural connection.
- Connection is important because it allows good things to follow.
- There are three elements for developing strong connections with your grandchildren:
  - Feeling emotionally close to each other – a special relationship that is mutually beneficial.
  - Regular contact – even if you're not physically near each other.
  - Being a source of social support – your grandchild knowing that you are always available to them and you are a safe space.

Individual reflection (5 min). How connected do you feel to your grandchildren?

Discussion questions (10–15 min).
- How do you connect with your grandchildren?
- What makes connecting with grandchildren tricky? Have you found ways to overcome that?
- Thinking about someone you feel connected to now, do you recognise the three elements for building strong connection in your relationship – emotional closeness, regular contact and being a source of social support?

Bible study (10–15 min). God made us for connection with each other – and we flourish when we are connected. Look at some or all of the following passages. What do they say about the power and value of connection?
- Genesis 2:18
- 1 Corinthians 13:6–7
- Proverbs 12:18
- Ecclesiastes 4:9–12
- 1 Peter 4:8
- 1 Thessalonians 5:11

Next steps (5 minutes). Allow people time to think about one or two things they want to take away or try from this session. A couple of ideas to suggest: for each grandchild, pick one thing you can do to let them know that you love them and are for them, or surprise each grandchild by getting in touch unexpectedly.

Pray for each other and each other's grandchildren (5–10 min).

Chapter 3: No one said it would be easy

Gather (5–15 min). A chance to catch up and share a cuppa.

Welcome and recap (5–10 min). Welcome and introduce anyone new. Recap the previous session and ask for any feedback. Did anyone try any new ways to connect with their grandchildren, or do something different?

Opening question (5–10 min). What's the hardest thing about being a grandparent?

Share the key ideas from the chapter (5 min).
- Grandparenting isn't as straightforward as parenting and you can feel powerless or confused.
- There are all sorts of scenarios that can make grandparenting tricky, including differences about faith.
- We looked at ideas for what to do:
  - when your adult children don't share your faith
  - when faith is an issue
  - when contact is hard
  - when your family's in pain
  - when you are struggling.

Individual reflection (5 min). What tricky situations am I facing as a grandparent?

Discussion questions (10–15 min). Choose one or more of the questions to help people explore the ideas further.

- 'What they explained was this: parenting is hard enough but grandparenting is a whole different ball game' (see page 39). Do you agree?
- Have you experienced any of the situations described in this chapter – or any we've not covered?
- What encouragement would you give to a grandparent who is finding things hard?

Bible study (10–15 min). Many people in the Bible faced tricky times. Have a look at some or all of these Bible passages. Are they helpful? Would you add any others?

- John 16:33
- Job 28:24
- Psalm 34:18
- Isaiah 41:10
- Mark 4:26–29
- Romans 8:26–27

Next steps (5 min). Allow people time to think about one or two things they want to take away or try from this session. Ideas to suggest: ask God for a next step for the tricky situation you are facing, or that people pair up and commit to praying for each other's situation between now and the next session.

Pray for each other and each other's grandchildren (5–10 min).

Chapter 4: Pray, pray, pray

Gather (5–15 min). A chance to catch up and share a cuppa.

Welcome and recap (5–10 min). Welcome and introduce anyone new. Recap the previous session and ask for any feedback. Does anyone have an update on a tricky situation they are facing in their family?

Opening question (5–10 min). Did your grandparents pray for you? What difference do you think it made?

Share the key ideas from the chapter (5 min).
- Prayer is the gift God has given us to help make a difference.
- Whatever the situation, you can pray.
- Bible pictures of prayer:
  - Jairus – you can bring your grandchildren to Jesus
  - Ezekiel – you can stand in the gap for grandchildren who don't know God
  - the widow – keep on praying
  - Elisha's servant – you can't always see what God is doing.
- Ideas of how to pray from grandparents.

Individual reflection (5 min). Which of the Bible pictures of prayer do you find encouraging?

Discussion questions (10–15 min). Choose one or more of the questions to help people explore the ideas further:

- What sort of 'pray-er' are you? Systematic? As you go? A list maker? A chatterer?
- Do your grandchildren know you pray for them? What difference does it or might it make if they know that you pray for them?
- Did you like any of the ideas from grandparents about ways to help pray for grandchildren?

Bible study (10–15 min). In Luke 11:1–11, Jesus teaches his disciples about how to pray. What stands out to you as you think about how to pray for your grandchildren?

Next steps (5 min). Allow people time to think about one or two things they want to take away or try from this session. An idea to suggest: pick one or more of the ideas at the end of the chapter for praying for your grandchildren to try.

Pray for each other and each other's grandchildren (5–10 min).

Chapter 5: Giving them glimpses of God

Gather (5–15 min). A chance to catch up and share a cuppa.

Welcome and recap (5–10 min). Welcome and introduce anyone new. Recap the previous session and ask for any feedback. Did anyone try any of the ideas for praying for their grandchildren? Were any of the Bible pictures of prayer we looked at last week helpful?

Opening question (5–10 min). What bits of your life with God are hidden from other people?

Share the key ideas from the chapter (5 min).
- If grandchildren don't understand who God is, why would they take notice of him?
- We want people to know Christianity isn't a set of activities but a relationship with God who has so much for them.
- We can 'create windows' into our relationship with God so grandchildren know what a relationship with God is like and how and why they would want to have one themselves.
- Three ideas for giving them glimpses of God:
  - add God into your ordinary conversations
  - do what you do with God in front of them
  - tell stories of you and God.
- There's a short video at **parentingforfaith.org/creating-windows** summarising the idea of creating windows.

Individual reflection (5 min). Who 'introduced' you to

God – who helped you see God as a person who was interested in you and loved you? How did they do that?

Discussion questions (10–15 min). Choose one or more of the questions to help people explore the ideas further.
- Thinking about Christians you know, what glimpses have you seen of their life with God that have inspired you?
- What do you do with God that you would like your grandchildren to know about?
- Do you think your grandchildren know that God is real and makes a difference to your life?

Bible study (10–15 min). Paul created windows into his life with God when he was writing to churches. Look at some or all of the following passages and see if you can identify what he was creating a window into and wonder at the impact this might have had on his readers.
- 2 Timothy 3:10–11
- 1 Corinthians 2:1–5
- Romans 7:14–25
- 1 Corinthians 9:19–23
- 2 Corinthians 12:1–10

Next steps (5 min). Allow people time to think about one or two things they want to take away or try from this session. An idea to suggest: pick one of the three ways to create windows – add God into your conversations; do what you do with God in front of them; tell stories of you and God – and use it with a grandchild or someone else.

Pray for each other and each other's grandchildren (5–10 min).

Chapter 6: Making sense of life

Gather (5–15 min). A chance to catch up and share a cuppa.

Welcome and recap (5–10 min). Welcome and introduce anyone new. Recap the previous session and ask for any feedback. Did anyone try creating a window into their relationship with God with a grandchild (or someone else)? What did they do and what happened?

Opening question (5–10 min). Have you ever been to a place or in a situation where everything was new and you needed help to figure it out? Who helped you?

Share the key ideas from the chapter (5 min).
- Grandchildren need to know how God fits into life, or he won't make sense and they won't see his relevance.
- Framing – explaining – is helping them see who God is and what he's doing – like being their guide on a journey.
- Four ideas for how to frame:
  - explain everything – adding in who God is or what he's doing
  - answer questions well
  - jumpstart conversations about God
  - lay foundations for their future.
- There's a short video at **parentingforfaith.org/framing** summarising the idea of framing.

Individual reflection (5 min). What have you helped your grandchildren understand? How did you do that? For example, how to change a nappy, fix their bike, flip a pancake, deal with a strong emotion or solve a problem?

Discussion questions (10–15 min). Choose one or more of the questions to help people explore the ideas further.

- How does knowing about God help you make sense of the world?
- What do you think your grandchildren need to understand about God?
- Is there anything coming up in your grandchildren's lives that you might want to frame for them, so they have an idea of where God will be and what he will be doing?
- What questions do they have about God and the world?

If you have time, you could try answering a question using the four steps outlined in the chapter. People might have a question or use one of the following: What does God look like? Does God do miracles today? Does God get sad?

Bible study (10–15 minutes). God gives Mary a spiritual framework that will enable her to be Jesus' mother and handle all that this will bring. What do the following passages tell us about how he does that?

- Luke 1:26–38
- Luke 1:39–45
- Luke 2:22–35
- Luke 2:41–52

Next steps (5 min). Allow people time to think about one or two things they want to take away or try from this session. An idea to suggest: pick one of the three ways to frame and have a go with a grandchild or someone else.

Pray for each other and each other's grandchildren (5–10 min).

Chapter 7: Getting to grips with God

Gather (5–15 min). A chance to catch up and share a cuppa.

Welcome and recap (5–10 min). Welcome and introduce anyone new. Recap the previous session and ask for any feedback. Did anyone try any of the ideas for framing – or explaining – who God is with their grandchildren or someone else? What happened?

Opening question (5–10 min). Can you think of anyone – a friend, family member or a public figure – where your view of them has changed over the years? What happened to change your view of them?

Share the key ideas from the chapter (5 min).
- How we feel about someone affects our relationship with them.
- We're all on a journey of getting to know God better and better.
- Grandchildren get their ideas about God from many places and may have some tangled views.
- You can help them build a broad and balanced view of God, as well as unwinding tangled views you spot.
- It's not about being an expert but sharing what you know about God.

Individual reflection (5 min). How would you describe God using only three words? When you look at those three words, what picture of God do they paint? Is anything missing? What words might you add to give a fuller picture of God?

Discussion questions (10–15 min). Choose one or more of the questions to help people explore the ideas further.

- Where do you think your grandchildren get their ideas about God from?
- Which of the ideas for broadening their view of God do you like: deliberately adding balance; digging into Bible stories; asking questions with no right answers? Which might you use?
- Have you noticed any mixed-up views of God in your grandchildren? How might you unwind them?
- If it's helpful, there's a short video at **parentingforfaith. org/unwinding** summarising the idea of unwinding wrong views of God.

Bible study (10–15 min). As a group, how many names of God can you recall? What does your list tell you about God? Look at Exodus 3:13–14. Why, given that God has so many names, does he give the answer he does?

Next steps (5 min). Allow people time to think about one or two things they want to take away or try from this session. Some ideas to suggest: spend time with God chatting about each of your grandchildren. Ask him if there's anything that grandchild needs to understand about him. Then ask God for your next step. If it's helpful there's a free download of '101 ways to start a conversation with God' available at **parentingforfaith.org/101-conversations**.

Pray for each other and each other's grandchildren (5–10 min).

Chapter 8: Seeing God in the Bible

If you can, borrow a range of Bible storybooks and Bibles for children and teens and bring them to this session for the group to look at.

Gather (5–15 min). A chance to catch up and share a cuppa.

Welcome and recap (5–10 min). Welcome and introduce anyone new. Recap the previous session and ask for any feedback. Did anyone spotted any tangled views of God in their grandchildren, or have a go at starting an interesting conversation about God?

Opening question (5–10 min). What stories or passages from the Bible are particularly significant for you? Why? What do they help you see about God?

Share the key ideas from the chapter (5 min).
- Asaph tells us in Psalm 78 that stories about God are powerful ways to help people understand exactly who God is and why we should trust him.
- There's a big story of the Bible people need to know but many people think the Bible is just a lot of little stories or just a source of moral truth.
- Ways to share the Bible with grandchildren so they see the big story of God:
  - choose Bibles and Bible storybooks well
  - share Bible stories well
  - help them see that the God of the Bible is the same today.

Individual reflection (5 min). How has the Bible helped you understand God and put your trust in him? What lessons from the Bible would you like your grandchildren to know?

Discussion questions (10–15 min). Choose one or more of the questions to help people explore the ideas further.
- What is your grandchildren's experience of the Bible?
- Have you shared the Bible with your grandchildren? How have you done this? Any top tips?
- Can you think of Bible stories you might want to share if a grandchildren is facing injustice, a big change or fear?

If you have time, why not, as a group, have a go at retelling one of the following Bible stories, adding in pauses to ask what God might have been doing, thinking or feeling: Jesus walking on the water (Matthew 14:22–33); Naomi and Ruth (Ruth 1:1–18); David and Goliath (1 Samuel 17:20–50).

Bible study (10–15 min). Read the following, familiar Bible stories – or others of your choice – and as you do so, consider what they teach us about God and how that is relevant today.
- Hannah in the tabernacle (1 Samuel 1:1–19)
- Saul's conversion (Acts 9:1–19)
- The fall (Genesis 3:1–24)

Next steps (5 min). Allow people time to think about one or two things they want to take away or try from this session. An idea to suggest: try with a grandchild one of the ideas for choosing Bible storybooks and Bibles well.

Pray for each other and each other's grandchildren (5–10 min).

Chapter 9: Moving from head to heart

Gather (5–15 min). A chance to catch up and share a cuppa.

Welcome and recap (5–10 min). Welcome and introduce anyone new. Recap the previous session and ask for any feedback. Did anyone try any of the ideas for sharing the Bible well with grandchildren? What did they do and what happened?

Opening question (5–10 min). Do you think your grandchildren know God as a friend, or just know *about* him?

Share the key ideas from the chapter (5 min).
- The Bible shows that it is God's intention that we can be his friends and that we can 'connect' with him.
- The big story of the Bible is all about how God restores that connection after it is broken when sin comes into the world at the fall.
- Connection with God allows us to experience so many good things: God as our father, comforter, guide and much, much more.
- We can help grandchildren see and understand our connection with God.
- We can help them understand what prayer is and create windows into how we pray so they can see it and try it for themselves.

Individual reflection (5 min). When do you feel closest to God? What helps you connect with him?

Discussion questions (10–15 min). Choose one or more of the questions to help people explore the ideas further.
- What would you like your grandchildren to understand about why connecting with God is important?
- How could you create windows into or frame how you and God connect – what makes you feel close to him and able to draw on his strength, comfort and wisdom?
- Do your grandchildren pray? How could you help them know what prayer is for you?

Bible study (10–15 min). As Christians we have received the gift of God the Holy Spirit, with whom we are deeply connected. What do the following passages tell us of the things that connection brings us? (Note that the word 'advocate' used in John can also mean 'comforter' or 'helper').
- John 14:26; 16:7
- Acts 1:8
- Romans 5:5; 8:26; 15:13
- 1 Corinthians 12:4
- Ephesians 1:17

Next steps (5 min). Allow people time to think about one or two things they want to take away or try from this session. Some ideas to suggest: if you think your grandchildren may not realise we can connect with God, try one of the ideas for introducing the idea and seeing what it is like. Or think about how you could create opportunities for your grandchildren to pray and if you can, have a go.

Pray for each other and each other's grandchildren (5–10 min).

Chapter 10: Opening up the Tardis

As this is the last session, you might want to ask people to think about how they want to continue this journey of helping their grandchildren meet and know God. Could the group carry on meeting? Are there other things they would like to explore or do to help and encourage each other?

Gather (5–15 min). A chance to catch up and share a cuppa.

Welcome and recap (5–10 min). Welcome and introduce anyone new. Recap the previous session and ask for any feedback. Did anyone try any of the ideas for helping their grandchildren connect, or giving them opportunities to pray. What did they do and what happened?

Opening question (5–10 min). What is it about church that you love?

Share the key ideas from the chapter (5 minutes).
- Church is like the Tardis – so much more on the inside than most people think.
- You can help grandchildren see what you love about church – so they realise it's interesting, powerful and a possibility for them too.
- Ways to create windows into and frame the importance of church for you:
  - when you talk about church, add in the God bits
  - add the 'whys' – explaining what doing the activity of church means to you

- Make visits to church count:
  - do your preparation
  - help the service make sense and point out what God is doing
  - do what you do with God
  - debrief afterwards.

Individual reflection (5 min). What would you love your grandchildren to realise about church?

Discussion questions (10–15 min). Choose one or more of the questions to help people explore the ideas further.
- Were you taken to church by a grandparent, or have you taken a grandchild to church? What was it like?
- Do you think your grandchildren know that church is 'interesting, powerful and a possibility for them too' (see page 146)?
- How could you create windows into or frame the importance of church for you?
- If you take your grandchildren to church, which of the ideas in this chapter might you want to try?

Bible study (10–15 min). The Bible gives us some descriptions of the impact of the early church. What do the following passages reveal? Do you recognise the same in your church?
- Acts 2:42–43
- 2 Corinthians 8:1–4
- Acts 4:32–35
- Acts 2:46–47
- Acts 6:1–6
- Acts 9:36–41

Next steps (5 min). Allow people time to think about one or two things they want to take away or try from this session. Some ideas to suggest: think about what you'd like your grandchildren to understand about church. What ideas from this from this chapter might help you show them that? Or, if you take your grandchildren to church, try one or two ideas from the section 'Making visits to church count'.

Pray for each other and each other's grandchildren (5–10 min).

Notes

1 See, for example, Luke 5:16; John 9; Mark 9:33–37; 8:34ff; 2:15; Luke 9:51–52; Matthew 5; Mark 12:13; Luke 22:9

2 See Judges 6:11; Genesis 18:1; 1 Samuel 3:3; Judges 13:9; Acts 10:10; Genesis 21:16; Exodus 3:1

3 See, for example, Ann Buchanan and Julia Griggs, 'The impact of grandparental involvement on child well-being', *'My Second Mum and Dad': The involvement of grandparents in the lives of teenage grandchildren*, research report (Grandparents Plus, August 2009), **kinship.org.uk/wp-content/uploads/2020/02/My-Second-Mum-and-Dad-research-report.pdf**; Ann Buchanan and Anna Rotkirch, 'Twenty-first century grandparents: global perspectives on changing roles and consequences', *Contemporary Social Science* 13.2 (2018), pp. 131–44, **doi.org/10.1080/21582041.2018.1467034**; Sara M. Moorman, Jeffrey E. Stokes, 'Solidarity in the grandparent–adult grandchild relationship and trajectories of depressive symptoms', *The Gerontologist* 56.3 (June 2016), pp. 408–20, **doi.org/10.1093/geront/gnu056**.

4 Quoted in David J. Bredehoft, 'When grandparents undermine parents' rules', *Psychology Today*, 1 October 2020, **psychologytoday.com/gb/blog/the-age-overindulgence/202010/when-grandparents-undermine-parents-rules**.

5 2 Timothy 1:5; Genesis 24:67; Genesis 48; Ruth 4:16.

6 Vern L. Bengtson, Norella M. Putney and Susan Harris, *Families and Faith: How religion is passed down across generations* (Oxford University Press, 2013).

7 Youth for Christ, 'Gen Z: Rethinking culture', p. 33, **indd.adobe.com/view/0672cab6-cf26-4595-b572-9146f31af43e**. For other research, see Matthew Deprez, 'Grandparents influencing faith in

194

grandkids', The D6 Podcast, episode 121, 20 August 2018, **d6family. com/podcast/121-grandparents-influencing-faith-in-grandkids- matthew-deprez**; and Matthew Deprez, 'The role of grandparents in shaping faith formation of grandchildren: a case study', *Christian Education Journal* 14.1 (2017), pp. 109–27, **doi.org/10.1177/073989131701400110.**

8 Susan Longhurst, '"Who joins the Catholic Church and why?" Exploring the nature of Catholic conversion for individuals in the Archdiocese of Southwark', PhD thesis, St Mary's University, 2022, **research.stmarys.ac.uk/id/eprint/5539.**

9 Buchanan and Griggs, *'My Second Mum and Dad'*, p. 13.

10 S.E. Holmes, 'Excluded or part of the team? Investigating of the role of grandparents in Christian faith nurture, using discourse analysis', *Review of Religious Research* 64 (2022), pp. 829–51, **doi.org/10.1007/s13644-022-00520-2.**

11 See Rita Brhel, 'The vital importance of the grandparent–grandchild bond', *The Attached Family*, 31 July 2013, **theattachedfamily.com/membersonly/?p=164**, citing M. Silverstein and S. Ruiz, 'Breaking the chain: how grandparents moderate the transmission of maternal depression to their grandchildren', *Family Relations*, 55 (2006), pp. 601–12.

12 Tim and Darcy Kimmel, *Extreme Grandparenting: The ride of your life* (Tyndale House, 2007), p. 128.

13 Psalm 46:1.

14 Buchanan and Griggs, *'My Second Mum and Dad'*, ch. 7; Buchanan and Rotkirch, 'Twenty-first century grandparents', p. 137.

15 Anita Cleverley, *Faithful Grandparents: Hope and love through the generations* (BRF, 2019), p. 134.

16 See Jonah 2:1; Genesis 32:22–30; Mark 1:35; Romans 8:26–27; 1 Samuel 1:10; Judges 5; Genesis 18:16–33; Judges 6:11–17.

17 Rachel Turner, *Parenting Children for a Life of Faith: Helping children meet and know God*, omnibus edition (BRF, 2018), p. 26.

18 See Psalm 23:1; Genesis 22:14; Psalm 57:2; Judges 6:24; Psalm 19:14; Isaiah 33:22.

19 See 1 Kings 19:12; Ruth 4:18–22; Luke 10:38–42.

20 Revelation 22:13; Genesis 16:13; Psalm 89:8 ('Lord of the angel armies' is translated as 'Lord God Almighty' in the NIV); Exodus 15:26.

21 Judges 6; Zephaniah 3:17; Jonah 1:1, 3:1–2, 4:11.

22 Turner, *Parenting Children for a Life of Faith*. See especially chapters 4 and 5.

196 GRANDPARENTING FOR FAITH

23 See John 3:16; 1 John 4:9–10, 12; Matthew 28:20; Ezekiel 34:11; Luke 15:6; Philippians 2:12–13; Genesis 1:26–30.
24 See Exodus 3:3, 6, 11; 4:1.
25 For example, Samuel (1 Samuel 3:20–21), Aaron (Numbers 18:1–24) and Solomon (1 Kings 3).
26 See Ephesians 2:18; John 14:15–17, 26; Romans 5:5; 8:26; John 16:12–15; Acts 9:31.
27 For an explanation of arrow prayers, see **prayerideas.org/using-powerful-quick-arrow-prayers.**
28 See Philippians 4:7; 1 Peter 5:7; Matthew 10:29–31.
29 See Luke 6:12; 2 Kings 19:14–19; 1 Samuel 1:1–19; Nehemiah 2:4–5; Judges 5; Genesis 18:16–33; 32:22–32.
30 'Equipping grandparents', Lunch with Leaders Parenting for Faith Facebook Live session, 24 May 2023, **facebook.com/watch/live/?ref=watch_permalink&v=252541734096916** (at 22:30 minutes).
31 See John 10:2–5; Jeremiah 33:3.

Acknowledgements

My daughter Hannah, who believes unfailingly in me and who always cheers me on and brings me cups of tea – thank you!

Rachel Turner, who told me I could write a book, shouted loud her encouragement and gave freely of her wisdom – thank you for your belief in me. You have changed me!

My sister Sarah and my dear friend Kirsty – for listening, laughing and being there. I am grateful for you both.

The Parenting for Faith team – Anna, Iona, Kate and Lucy – working alongside you is truly a privilege and joy. Thank you for being so generous with your time and your love.

The wider BRF team for their support, expertise and kindness.

Bill Lattimer and Caroline Montgomery, for your commitment to Parenting for Faith over many years, and for your kind and gentle guidance and wisdom.

The grandparent groups in Devizes and Chipping Campden who piloted a lot of this material. Thank you for going on a journey of discovery with us.

The grandparents we interviewed for this book and the 321 grandchildren who answered our survey – you have helped to shape this book and given me valuable insights into the reality of being a grandparent, and being a grandparent of faith, as well as providing the quotations scattered throughout the chapters.

parenting for faith®

Do you hope to raise children and teens who stay connected to God throughout their life's journey? The good news is you can! We believe God has placed you in the perfect position to do just that. We'd love you to be part of our supportive community of parents, extended family members, carers and church leaders, so you can find exactly the help and encouragement you're looking for, 24/7.

Find us on social media

 facebook.com/parentingforfaithBRF

 twitter.com/godconnected

 instagram.com/parentingforfaithbrf

 youtube.com/brfcharity

Ministries

Inspiring people of all ages to grow in Christian faith

BRF Ministries is the home of Anna Chaplaincy, Living Faith, Messy Church and Parenting for Faith

As a charity, our work would not be possible without fundraising and gifts in wills.
To find out more and to donate,
visit brf.org.uk/give or call +44 (0)1235 462305